A GUIDE TO
PACEM IN TERRIS
FOR STUDENTS

A Guide To Pacem in Terris For Students

AN ORIGINAL DEUS BOOK

by
PETER RIGA

(With Discussion Questions)

DEUS BOOKS
Paulist Press
(Paulist Fathers)
Glen Rock, N.J.

NIHIL OBSTAT: Daniel V. Flynn, J.C.D.
Censor Librorum

IMPRIMATUR: ✠ Francis Cardinal Spellman
Archbishop of New York

June 25, 1964

The Nihil Obstat and Imprimatur are official declarations that a book or pamphlet is free of doctrinal or moral error. No implication is contained therein that those who have granted the Nihil Obstat and Imprimatur agree with the contents, opinions or statements expressed.

Library of Congress
Catalog Card Number: 64-24515

COVER DESIGN: Claude Ponsot

Published by the Paulist Press
Editorial Office: 401 W. 59th St., N.Y. 19, N.Y.
Business Office: Glen Rock, New Jersey

Manufactured in the
United States of America

24

TO THE BELOVED MEMORY OF
JOHN F. KENNEDY

"Blessed are the peacemakers, for
they shall be called sons of God"
(Matthew 5, 9)

Contents

7

Introduction

IN HIS MAGNIFICENT encyclical on the social teachings of the Church, *Mater et Magistra,* the beloved Pope John XXIII made the following statement:

222. Above all, we affirm that the social teaching proclaimed by the Catholic Church cannot be separated from her traditional teaching regarding man's life.

223. Wherefore, it is our earnest wish that more and more attention be given to this branch of learning. First of all, we urge that attention be given to such studies in Catholic schools on all levels, and especially in seminaries, although we are not unaware that in some of these latter institutions this is already being done admirably. . . . (*Mater et Magistra*).

The Holy Father is simply saying that our Christian practice is not complete nor total without the social teachings of the Church. Christian life is composed of two most important elements; one without the other makes our profession of Christ false and sinful:

1. God has revealed Himself in Christ, our Lord: "God so loved the world that He gave His only begotten son" (John 3, 16). God so loved man that He wants to share His life and love with us through Christ. Redeemed and saved by Christ, we now live the life of the Resurrection of Christ. We are God's family, God's children in the real meaning of this word. This message of love comes to us today in the Church, the community of God's love and into which we have been born as members through Baptism. But this is only half of the story.

2. The other half is that we must *live* as sons of God; we must practice the love that God has given us: "I have given you an example . . . that you love one another" (John 13, 15-34). Love is proven only by action—how we treat and respect each other. If I say I love my fellow man and do not attempt to feed him if he is hungry, can I really say that I love that man? We would say that my love is not real, that it is only empty words. So, too, in Christianity, we must attempt with all our energy and talent to be of service, to help our fellow man in all of his troubles and difficulties. To the poor, we must attempt to bring comfort and to improve his financial situation; to the Negro, we must attempt to help him procure all of his God-given rights; to the underdeveloped nations, we must attempt to give all the material and economic assistance possible. It is only in this way that our love for Christ can be proven here on earth.

St. John tells us that if we say we love Christ and do not attempt to help His children (who are our brothers in Christ) then we are liars and our Christianity is a big lie. Pope John, in one of his last talks before he died, called this attitude a hypocrisy and a denial of Christ.

That is the reason the Holy Father wants the social doctrine of the Church taught in every type of school in all of the Catholic world. That is the reason he wants his sons and daughters in the Church to become acquainted with this thought of the Church even from their earliest years; and this is the reason why this commentary on one of Pope John's encyclicals called *Peace on Earth* has been written. If students today are not acquainted with the Church's teachings in this matter, then neither will the Catholic adults of tomorrow know any more about it.

What is this social teaching of the Church? It is hard to put it in just a few words because it covers so many different subjects. Briefly, we can say that it is the teaching of Christ on how we are to live our lives in the world as men and as Christians. Man is not like a piece of paper that you can neatly divide into two separate parts: man is one, and the Christian is one whether he prays or whether he works in an office.

Our Lord does care how he works in an office, for the Christian must work as Christ would have worked. He prays as Christ would have prayed. If this is so, then the Christian must know *how* Christ would have worked in an office, or a union, or a school, or a factory. In all of these worldly matters, the Christian must have the mind of Christ. This is what is given to us in the social teachings of the Catholic Church. They reflect the mind of Christ on the affairs of men in the world. It is, therefore, of the greatest importance that we learn it, and more important, that we practice it in our daily lives. Otherwise, we shall live, in the words of Pope John, a big lie.

The encyclical (letter) *Peace on Earth* of Pope John XXIII is one of the best ways we have of discovering what is the mind of Christ in many of these affairs of men in the world. The Holy Father discusses such things as peace, under-developed countries, law, atomic bombs, the United Nations, freedom of worship, democracy, and many other subjects that are of great interest to man all over the world. They are of even greater interest to Catholics, since the Pope tells us clearly what Christ thinks of each of these sub-jects and, consequently, what we must think of them. If we learn this doctrine and practice it, we shall be, as our Lord describes us, "the light of the World" and we shall help bring about true peace in a world that knows only war and hatred.

One last word. Once you have learned this doctrine and begun to practice it, you must be prepared for great suffering. There are many men who do not agree with Christ and conse-quently, they will not agree with you. You will be opposed and perhaps persecuted for these be-liefs. This should not discourage you in the least. After all, they crucified our Lord for what He believed in; can you expect anything less?

In suffering for Christ's teaching, you will become more and more like Christ since it is by suffering that we become like our Lord. "Blessed are you when men reproach you and persecute you, and speaking falsely, say all manner of evil against you, for my sake. Rejoice and exult, because your reward is great in heaven (Matt. 5, 12). The Christian must always be Christ to the world, and like Christ be crucified again with Him.

To follow Christ is not an easy thing; it is not for weaklings; it takes great courage, courage that is given to us by the Holy Spirit who dwells in our hearts through the sacraments of Baptism and Confirmation. We have nothing to fear for He is with us all days. That is the reason it is so very important to pray always to the Holy Spirit to enlighten us for what we must do and to strengthen us for what must be done for Christ.

The encyclical *Peace on Earth* is divided into five parts. Each one is built on the other, much like a house is built on its foundation. We shall try to follow the Holy Father as he builds this edifice of peace. We shall first give the words of the Holy Father and then explain what he means. We must always remember that, in reality, it is Christ who speaks to us through the words of His Vicar. In this way, we shall come to understand the mind of Christ in all subjects that the Holy Father is going to discuss.

The subject matter of this encyclical letter of the Pope is important for another reason. The Second Vatican Council is discussing these same subjects in order to make the Church's influence felt in the world of our day. As Pope Paul VI has said, the message of the Church must be brought to the problems of the men of our day. Only the Church can really do it. Therefore, how very important it is for Catholics to, first of all, understand fully what the message of the Church is to the modern world, and then to put it into practice with our whole hearts and souls.

PART 1
The Order
Between Men

ENCYCLICAL LETTER OF
HIS HOLINESS, JOHN XXIII
BY DIVINE PROVIDENCE POPE

To the Venerable Brothers
the Patriarchs, Primates,
Archbishops, Bishops
and Other Local Ordinaries
in Peace and Communion
with the Apostolic See,
to the Clergy and Faithful
of the Whole World and
to All Men of Good Will:

On Establishing Universal Peace
in Truth, Justice, Charity and Liberty.

POPE JOHN XXIII

VENERABLE BROTHERS AND BELOVED CHILDREN
HEALTH AND APOSTOLIC BENEDICTION

THIS INTRODUCTION to the encyclical is striking because for the first time the Holy Father addresses his words to the whole world, both Catholic and non-Catholic. What the Pope is going to say will hold good for all men, no matter who and where they are. Why is this? Because, since we are all created by God, we possess certain things in common. God has created us equal because He gave every person an immortal soul. God also gave every person an intellect, by which each man can understand what God wants him to do.

There are two ways we can come to know about God. One is by the Bible in which God has spoken directly to us through the prophets and above all, through Christ. The other is by our mind or our reason whereby we can understand what God has created. Just as I can know about another person, his talents, his difficulties, etc., by reading his biography, so, too, we can know something about God from the book that God has written — all of creation. This is what the Holy Father means in the following paragraphs of his encyclical. Men — all men — can learn many things about God by considering the book of nature that God Himself created at the beginning of time. The Holy Father continues along this line of thought:

2. The progress of learning and the inventions of technology clearly show that, both in living things and in the forces of nature, an astonishing order reigns, and they also bear witness to the greatness of man, who can understand that order and create suitable instruments to harness those forces of nature and use them to his benefit.

3. But the progress of science and the inventions of technology show above all the infinite greatness

of God, who created the universe and man himself. He created all things out of nothing, pouring into them the abundance of His wisdom and goodness, so that the holy psalmist praises God in these words: *O Lord, our Lord, how glorious is Your name over all the earth* (Ps. 8, 1). Elsewhere he says: *How manifold are Your works, O Lord! In Wisdom You have wrought them all* (Ps. 103, 24). God also created man in His own *image and likeness* (cf. Gen. 1, 26), endowed him with intelligence and freedom, and made him lord of creation, as the same psalmist declares in the words: *You have made him little less than the angels, and crowned him with glory and honor. You have given him rule over the works of your hands, putting all things under his feet* (Ps. 8, 6-7).

4. How strongly does the turmoil of individual men and peoples contrast with the perfect order of the universe! It is as if the relationships which bind them together could be controlled only by force.

5. But the Creator of the world has imprinted in man's heart an order which his conscience reveals to him and enjoins him to obey: *They show the work of the Law written in their hearts. Their conscience bears witness to them* (Rom. 2, 15). And how could it be otherwise? For whatever God has made shows forth His infinite wisdom, and it is manifested more clearly in the things which have greater perfection.

So what the Holy Father is going to say is not simply for Catholics, but for all men. He appeals to their reason and to their good will. There are many men in this world who are not of our faith but who are sincere and good men who want peace and human dignity with all of their hearts. The Pope respects them and wants to co-operate with them in any way he can. This ought also to be our attitude to all men of good will, no matter what their faith might be. The Pope will discuss this even more in the last part of the encyclical. The Holy Father emphasizes this point when he says:

Peace on Earth, which men of every era have so eagerly yearned for, can be firmly established only if the order laid down by God be dutifully observed.

The only way men shall find peace in this world is by carefully observing what God wishes. No peace can come to men as long as they disobey His commands. But just what are these commands of God that men must obey if they are to have peace here on earth? The encyclical will explain what each of these commands are. That is the reason the Holy Father is writing this encyclical at a time when there is no peace. In today's world, men hate and are preparing to kill each other with weapons so great and so powerful that all human life may disappear from the earth. Therefore, we can see how terribly important are the words of the Pope and how seriously we ought to listen to them and put them into action. This may be the last chance for men to listen to God and to have true peace.

But the Holy Father is optimistic. He has great hopes that, aided by God's grace, man can if he wants, obey God and thereby find true peace. There are some men who say that man

can do nothing to avoid war and hunger; the
Pope does not agree with them. The Holy Father
is saying the same thing as St. Paul when this
great Apostle said: "I can do all things in him
who strengthens me" (Phil. 4, 5). With God's
grace and man's good will, peace can come to the
world. But man must follow God's will. The
Holy Father now goes on to give what exactly
God's will really is:

9. Any human society, if it is to be well-ordered
and productive, must lay down as a foundation this
principle: that every human being is a person; his
nature is endowed with intelligence and free will.
By virtue of this, he has rights and duties of his own,
flowing directly and simultaneously from his very
nature, which are therefore universal, inviolable
and inalienable.
10. If we look upon the dignity of the human person in the light of divinely revealed truth, we cannot
help but esteem it far more highly; for men are redeemed by the blood of Jesus Christ; they are by
grace the children and friends of God and heirs of
eternal glory.

When we come to the end of our reading of the
encyclical, we shall have noticed something very
strange: namely, that although the encyclical is
supposed to be about peace, the Holy Father continuously talks about the "rights of man." Why
is this? The answer is simple, for in order to have
any peace whatever, the rights of all men must be
promoted and safeguarded. This is the heart and
soul of true peace; and without it we not only

lack peace but we are slaves and not men. Why is this?

When God created man—and God creates every man who lives or ever will live—He created man in a much different way than He created the earth or the stars. The Bible says: "God created man in His image. In the image of God He created him" (Gen. 1, 27). This means that in each man there is something of God within him. It is this that gives man an infinite dignity over anything else in creation. And since this is so, we must respect and honor every man whom we meet as God's special creation, as God's child. Hence, we say that man has rights, that is, God has given him certain powers and abilities that no one, not even the Pope, can take away. All other men must not only respect these rights but also (if he is truly Christian) must see to it that each man's rights are given to him by other people and by the government.

As we shall see later, the government's principal job is to protect and promote these rights of men in any society. Any government that does not do this is called tyrannical and, in reality, is not a real government at all. So now we begin to understand what the Holy Father meant when he said that true peace will come only when men observe and obey God's teachings. The rights and the dignity of man is first in God's teachings.

11. Beginning our discussion of the rights of man, we see that every man has the right to life, to bodily integrity, and to the means which are necessary and

suitable for the proper development of life; these are primarily food, clothing, shelter, rest, medical care, and finally the necessary social services. Therefore a human being also has the right to security in cases of sickness, inability to work, widowhood, old age, unemployment, or in any other case in which he is deprived of the means of subsistence through no fault of his own.

What are some of these rights that man has? They are many indeed and the Holy Father goes on to number them all. The first of these are what we can call *economic rights*. God has created man both with a body and a soul. As a matter of fact, man is incomplete without his body as God has created him. This body of his has certain important needs without which a man would die: food, sleep, clothing, shelter, exercise, etc. God intended each man to have enough of these things because God has created man as body and as soul. Man on his part has a serious obligation to see to it that he acquires enough of these "economic" goods both for himself and his family. This is what the Holy Father means when he says that each man has a right to those economic necessities that are necessary for the life of his body.

But these are not the only rights man has. Man is not just a body, he also has a soul. He must, therefore, develop all of the talents and abilities that God has given him. He has a *right to an education* that will help him develop the talents God has given him. Man also has the right to enjoy the beauty of God's creation; therefore, he has a right to develop his artistic and cultural talents. Since man has a mind, he has the right to develop that mind by good, honest reading, by being able to read about both sides of a question. Other men in journalism and in the government have the obligation of telling their citizens the truth about local and world events. There is a final right that belongs to all men and is very important to them: the right to religious freedom. This is what the Holy Father has to say:

14. Every human being has the right to honor God according to the dictates of an upright conscience, and therefore the right to worship God privately and publicly.

What the Holy Father means is that every man, once he has made up his mind on how God is to be worshiped, has the right to worship God in that way. This does not mean that we are free to worship God in any way we want; in reality, we must endeavor to find out how God wants us to worship Him, for He is God and we are His children. We of the Catholic faith are very fortunate since we know and believe God speaks to us in His Church. By worshiping God in this Church, we are pleasing to Him.

But not all men are as fortunate as we. Some have been born into different religions and some into none. They sincerely think that they are following God's will in worshiping Him in that religion. They are in error, yes; but because they

are sincere, they have the right to worship God
according to what they believe is the truth.

The reason for this is not hard to understand.
Since we must worship God, above all, with our
hearts and souls, this worship must come from
our free will and our minds. If a man has sincerely searched for what God wants and yet is
still in error (for example, a Buddhist or a Hindu)
he must still worship God as best he can. He,
therefore, has a right to worship God as best he
can with his heart and soul. Even if he is in error,
he has this right and we must respect it. Otherwise we should be guilty of trying to force a man
to do what his conscience says he cannot do. We
may say, then, that each man's conscience is the
voice of God speaking to him and he can never
disobey this conscience. This is what the Holy
Father means when he says that a man "has a
right to follow the dictates of an upright conscience." The Holy Father now continues his
discussion on rights when he says:

15. Human beings have the right to choose freely
the state of life which they prefer, and therefore
the right to establish a family, with equal rights
and duties for man and woman, and also the right
to follow a vocation to the priesthood or the religious life.

There is another important right that the Holy
Father points out: The right to follow one's vocation. What does this mean?

To understand this, we must understand that

when God created us, He created us all equal insofar as we all have an immortal soul. We are all children of God no matter what our race, color or creed. Yet, this does not mean that we all have the same talents and abilities. To some God gave more, to others less. One person can teach and another may have the ability to fix an automobile engine. We are all, in a sense, unequal in abilities. But God has given us all *something*, no matter how much or how little. We all have the right to develop what God has given us; not only do we have the right to do so, but we have the obligation to do so. Students who watch TV all of the time or do not study are not following Christ's will.

There is another thing. God also calls us to different vocations in life. This may be to be a good mother or father, or if God wills, to be a priest or religious. Each of us has the right to follow the vocation to which we are called, all for God's honor and glory. No one may force us to follow a vocation we do not wish to follow. But we must always remember that a vocation (to marriage or the religious life) is God's gift and we must use it for His honor and glory.

26. The dignity of the human person involves the right to take an active part in public affairs and to contribute one's part to the common good of the citizens. For, as Our Predecessor of happy memory, Pius XII, pointed out: *The human individual, far from being an object and, as it were, a merely passive element in the social order, is in fact, must be*

*and must continue to be, its subject, its foundation
and its end* (Cf. Radio Broadcast, Christmas Eve,
1944).

27. The human person is also entitled to a juridical
protection of his rights, a protection that should
be efficacious, impartial and inspired by the true
norms of justice. As our Predecessor Pius XII
teaches: *That perpetual privilege proper to man,
by which every individual has a claim to the protection of his rights, and by which there is assigned
to each a definite and particular sphere of rights,
immune from all arbitrary attacks, is the logical
consequence of the order of justice willed by God*
(Cf. Radio Broadcast, Christmas Eve, 1942) .

The rights of man of which we have been
speaking come from God and therefore nobody
can "grant" or "give" them to any other person.
God alone can give a man his rights. If anyone—
government or individual — should attempt to
take these rights away or make it difficult for some
men to use their rights, such action is what we
call immoral, that is, it is against the will of God.

Men, says the Holy Father, are *social* in nature.
What does he mean? He means that no man can
be born or grow up or feed himself or conduct
himself well without the cooperation of other
men. Men need each other in every way. Even
to be born, a man must have two parents who
must take care of him for many years since he is
not able to take care of himself.

And since man must live with his fellow man
in what we call society, we need laws to govern
and regulate these relations between men and be-

tween the governments that rule them. This is a very important point to note: The laws are good and just when they protect man and his rights; they are evil and harmful when they attempt to take away or lessen these rights of man. As a matter of fact, the Holy Father says that the principal work of the government is to protect and guarantee these rights.

In our country, these are written in the *Bill of Rights* which lists the rights and freedoms of each man and woman in the United States. These rights of man, when they are in the law, are called *civil rights* and the government must see to it that these civil rights are protected. Thus we can also read in the 14th amendment of the U.S. Constitution: "No state shall make or enforce any law which shall abridge [lessen] the privileges or immunities of citizens . . . nor shall any state deprive any person of life, liberty or property, without due process of law; nor deny to any person within its jurisdiction [territory] the equal protection of laws." This is exactly what the Holy Father means when he says that "the human person is also entitled to a juridical [in the laws] protection that should be efficacious [real], impartial [without regard to race, color or creed] and inspired by the true norms of justice."

If, for example, I am accused of a crime, say murder, I may have a public defense of my case before an impartial judge who shall judge the case only on the evidence before him. In our country we correctly say that a person is innocent until he is proven guilty beyond a reasonable doubt. This is good because most men are good and law-abiding; their lives, good name, and property must be protected against evil men who, because they have greater power, are sometimes tempted to take away these things from other weaker men. The law, when it is just, protects us all. It is "blind" when it does not take account of the color of our skin, or the creed we believe, or the race from which we come. Its decrees are just for everyone from the President of the United States to the humble ditchdigger. Now the Holy Father emphasizes another important point:

28. The natural rights with which We have been dealing are, however, inseparably connected, in the very person who is their subject, with just as many respective duties; and rights as well as duties find their source, their sustenance and their inviolability in the natural law which grants or enjoins them.
29. For example, the right of every man to life is correlative with the duty to preserve it; his right to a decent manner of living with the duty of living it becomingly; and his right to investigate the truth freely, with the duty of seeking it and of possessing it ever more completely and profoundly.

Man has rights. We have seen this already. But this is only one half of the story. If God has given men rights, He has also given them responsibilities that go along with every right man has. A man cannot just sit back and say, "I have a right to an education!" He must work to develop the

talents he has. In other words, he has an obligation to develop and work at what God has given
him. If he does not do this, he is acting immorally, that is, against the will of God. Therefore,
the rights and the talents God has given us are
not just for our comfort; they are invitations to
God's glory by developing and increasing them;
they are invitations to love our fellow men by
seeing to it that all men are given their rights
and have the opportunity to develop their talents.

Christianity means to give one's self to others
in self-sacrifice. If I have a talent for medicine,
I have the obligation to develop that talent.
Why? What is the true *Christian* answer? So
that I can give myself as a doctor to help those
in need. If my first wish is "to make a lot of
money," then I am not doing God's will. He has
given me this talent with which to help others,
my brothers and sisters, who are all men in need.
Our talents have been given to us *both* for our
personal fulfillment and the service of others.
But strange as it might seem, I can only fulfill
myself by helping others.

Our Lord said the same thing, "He who finds
his life will lose it, and he who loses his life for
my sake, will find it" (Matt. 10, 38). This is the
one law of Jesus Christ: that we love each other
by helping each other in any way we can. When
the doctor of the law asked Jesus who was his
neighbor, Jesus answered with the story of the
good Samaritan: anyone who is in need is my
brother. This is the reason the Holy Father can

say that all men must work together for each
other's good. Why? Because they are all brothers.
In this connection the Pope writes:

31. Since men are social by nature they are meant
to live with others and to work for one another's
welfare. A well-ordered human society requires
that men recognize and observe their mutual rights
and duties. It also demands that each contribute
generously to the establishment of a civic order in
which rights and duties are ever more sincerely and
effectively acknowledged and fulfilled.
32. It is not enough, for example, to acknowledge
and respect every man's right to the means of subsistence: one must also strive to obtain that he actually has enough in the way of food and nourishment.
33. The society of men must not only be organized
but must also provide them with abundant resources. This certainly requires that they observe
and recognize their mutual rights and duties; it also
requires that they collaborate together in the many
enterprises that modern civilization either allows
or encourages or demands.

And the Pope emphasizes this even more when
he makes the following statement:

35. A political society is to be considered well-
ordered, beneficial and in keeping with human
dignity if it is grounded on truth. As the Apostle
Paul exhorts us: *Wherefore, put away lying and
speak truth each one with his neighbor, because we
are members of one another* (Eph. 4, 25). This demands that reciprocal rights and duties be sincerely
recognized. Furthermore, human society will be
such as We have just described it, if the citizens,
guided by justice, apply themselves seriously to re-

specting the rights of others and discharging their
own duties; if they are moved by such fervor of
charity as to make their own the needs of others
and share with others their own goods; if, finally,
they work for a progressively closer fellowship in
the world of spiritual values. Human society is
realized in freedom, that is to say, in ways and means
in keeping with the dignity of its citizens, who accept the responsibility of their actions, precisely because they are by nature rational beings.

36. Human society, Venerable Brothers and beloved
children, ought to be regarded above all as a spiritual reality: in which men communicate knowledge
to each other in the light of truth; in which they
can enjoy their rights and fulfill their duties, and
are inspired to strive for moral good. Society should
enable men to share in and enjoy every legitimate
expression of beauty, and encourage them constantly to pass on to others all that is best in themselves,
while they strive to make their own the spiritual
achievements of others.

The Holy Father's view of government, the
State and of our society is inspiring. We can begin
to see what a great responsibility it is for the
Christian. Our religious duties, says the Pope,
do not end with services in the Church. This is
only one-half of the vocation of the true Christian. He must try to bring about a just political
and social order in the society in which he lives.
This means that each Catholic has the very serious obligation to work with all his talents to
bring about a just society. This is the other half
of his religious duty. If he fails in this second
obligation, or if he thinks that he can be a good
Catholic simply by going to Mass on Sunday and

receiving the sacraments once in a while, then he is sadly mistaken. This is only one-half of Christian holiness. The other half is our proof of our love of God and of our brothers by our acts, by trying to bring about the type of society which the Holy Father is describing here.

To be a statesman or a doctor or a lawyer or a businessman or a scientist, is not just to make a lot of money. Such an attitude is Christian treason. We become all of these things because Christ wants us to use these talents for the service of others. In the words of President Kennedy: "Do not ask what your country can do for you, but what you can do for your country." To make just laws or to heal the sick is what Christ wants. Every Christian has a vocation to use his talents and abilities for the service and love of others.

The Holy Father goes on to say that "Human society . . . ought to be regarded above all as a spiritual reality." It is sometimes hard for us to understand the meaning of the word "spiritual." Sometimes we think that this word is used in contrast or opposition to "material." This is not what the Pope means when he uses this word (and neither does the Bible). He means that society must be guided by the law of God which means justice and freedom for all of our fellow men throughout the world. He means a type of society where the rights of men (as we have already seen) are truly respected and protected and where true Christians strive with all their strength to see to it that, if this is not so, it will soon become so. This is the true test of whether a man is a true Christian or whether he is only half of one. It is very important that we realize that taking part in the society in which we live, to make it a better society in which to live for all men, is part and parcel of our Christian calling. The Pope emphasizes this point by saying:

37. The order which prevails in society is by nature moral. Grounded as it is in truth, it must function according to the norms of justice, it should be inspired and perfected by mutual love, and finally it should be brought to an ever more refined and human balance in freedom.

When the Pope uses the word "moral," he simply means that all of men's actions have a reference to God. As we have said, we cannot divide up a man and say: this part is a doctor, this part is religious and finally, this part belongs to the political order. No. A man is one just as a Christian is one. All of his actions must attempt to follow the will of God. Thus, when we say that the order that should prevail in society is moral, we mean that society in all of its parts is ruled by God's law and God's will. We must try continuously to find out what this law is.

The Holy Father gives us this law but only in a very general way. He sees society here on earth as an imperfect representation of what is to become perfect in eternal life. In other words, the Pope is giving Catholics a great responsibility. What is it? It is to attempt to bring about, with

God's help, a society which will reflect, at least to some degree, what we will have perfectly in heaven. In heaven, the society of men will be ruled with perfect justice; love will abound without measure and our freedom will be perfect because we have chosen God. So too, this is proposed by the Pope as a *model* for Christians to follow in building the society of men here on earth. We know that here on earth, this society will never be a perfect model of the society of men in heaven; but the Pope says, try with all of your hearts and all your energies.

But what rules or laws are we to follow in order to bring about this type of society? The first, as the Pope points out, is *truth*. This truth is that man is made in God's image and likeness and therefore is of infinite value or dignity. This will further bring about *justice* which is nothing more than giving each man his proper reward. Why is it? Why must we respect and help bring about this dignity of man?

Both truth and justice help us very little unless we have *love*. Love is to really and truly value each man as a man; to want him to become what God wants him to become; to want him to develop all the talents and abilities that God has given him. Love is not just sentiment or a lot of words; love is action to help our fellow man become what God wants him to become. If these conditions are fulfilled, then men will live in *freedom*, not fear or tyranny. When man's rights are not respected, loved and honored, man becomes a slave to other men or to the State. This is against the will of God who has created man free and to be loved.

39. Our age has three distinctive characteristics.

The Holy Father will now go on to develop three signs of the age ("characteristics") in which we live. These are very important to know and study because these three determine what kind of society we have now and will continue to have.

40. First of all, the working classes have gradually gained ground in economic and public affairs. They began by claiming their rights in the socio-economic sphere; they extended their action then to claims on the political level; and finally applied themselves to the acquisition of the benefits of a more refined culture. Today, therefore, workers all over the world refuse to be treated as if they were irrational objects without freedom, to be used at the arbitrary disposition of others. They insist that they be always regarded as men with a share in every sector of human society: in the social and economic sphere, in public life, and finally in the fields of learning and culture.

We cannot give the great teachings of the Church on economic affairs since this is too great a task for us here. But we can become more acquainted with this teaching of the Church by studying the following encyclicals: *Rerum Novarum* (1891) of Pope Leo XIII; *Quadragesimo Anno* (1931) of Pope Pius XI, and finally, *Mater et Magistra* (1961) of Pope John XXIII. Every Catholic should study this whole doctrine.

The Holy Father sums up this whole teaching in one short paragraph. The 19th century and the early part of the 20th were very hard for the workers of the United States and of the whole world. Times are not so difficult for us today in the United States, but this is only because our forefathers did much of the work to make our country as great and as strong as it is. Often, they had to fight and struggle for what we enjoy today —the Holy Father says that this is good.

However, this is not yet so all over the world. Many so-called "underdeveloped" countries are still struggling for these fundamental rights and the Holy Father praises them and encourages them in their struggle. Men all over the earth are becoming more and more aware that they have a perfect right to share in the material and economic goods that God created for all men.

41. Secondly, it is obvious to everyone that women are now taking a part in public life. This is happening more rapidly perhaps in nations of Christian civilization, and, more slowly but widely, among peoples who have inherited other traditions or cultures. Since women are becoming ever more conscious of their human dignity, they will not tolerate being treated as mere material instruments, but demand rights befitting a human person both in domestic and in public life.

Second, the new position of women in society is another important sign of the age in which we live. This was not always so—even in Christian countries. Still today, in certain Moslem and pagan countries, a woman is considered as little more than an animal whose only usefulness is to bring children into this world.

The Pope says that such a view of woman is not just. Christianity teaches that woman was created by God as was man and that therefore she is perfectly equal to man. Both of them are destined to live forever with God. But woman, even if she is equal to man, is different from man. That is, she has different qualities and abilities than does man. She is equal but different. These differences, says the Pope, are of great value for society. Each woman must attempt to develop her talents and abilities so that she, like man, can make her contribution to society as God wants her to make it. No one can accuse the Pope of any "narrow-mindedness" since he wants to extend to every man and woman on the face of the earth, his and her rights and duties.

42. Finally, the modern world, as compared with the recent past, has taken on an entirely new appearance in the field of social and political life. For since all nations have either achieved or are on the way to achieving independence, there will soon no longer exist a world divided into nations that rule others and nations that are subject to others.

Finally, the Holy Father looks with approval on the many new nations that have come into existence since the end of World War II. Over one billion of the earth's people have gained their independence since that time and the Pope praises their struggle for independence. These new nations were formerly colonies of the European countries and often were not treated fairly by them. As a matter of fact, many of these European nations used these colonies for their own wealth and power.

We must, however, be fair in our criticism of European colonialism in Africa and other parts of the world. We must remember the good that these European countries brought to these underdeveloped peoples. Such things as medical campaigns in North Africa, the establishment of many hospitals and medical centers, missionary schools and even universities (e.g. Lovanium in the Congo), dams and irrigation projects, etc. are all to their credit. Whenever we criticize either individuals or nations, we must be just and balanced. This, however, does not take away the many evils of the colonial system.

This can no longer be, explains the Holy Father, for the simple fact that every nation has the right to independence from other nations; each nation has the right to develop its natural resources so that its own people may live a more prosperous economic and social life. All men are equal just as all nations, because they are composed of men, are also equal. There is no nation that is superior to any other nation. Thus, the Church condemns what we call "racism," that is, the belief that one nation or people is better than another people or nation. Nothing could be further from Christian truth. This leads the Holy

Father into a very important question that we face as Americans:

44. On the contrary, the conviction that all men are equal by reason of their natural dignity has been generally accepted. Hence racial discrimination can in no way be justified, at least doctrinally or in theory. And this is of fundamental importance and significance for the formation of human society according to those principles which We have outlined above. For, if a man becomes conscious of his rights, he must become equally aware of his duties. Thus he who possesses certain rights has likewise the duty to claim those rights as marks of his dignity, while all others have the obligation to acknowledge those rights and respect them.

As we all know from our daily newspapers, the problem of the Negro is a very important one in our United States. There are certain men who say that some men are inferior to others, particularly the Negro. There are other men (Catholics as well) who, while not going this far, in practice say the same thing. They refuse to have Negroes live near them or go to school with them or let them have jobs for which the Negroes have ability. This is what we call the evil of discrimination. It is a sad and lamentable fact that many Christians practice such discrimination in their daily lives.

The teaching of the Holy Father and of the Church is very clear in this matter. Racial discrimination is a terrible evil and every effort must be made by all Christians not only to rid themselves of this evil, but to try to help Negroes attain their full rights as human beings and as American citizens. Lincoln freed the slaves more than one hundred years ago and still they are not free. As one famous American judge put it: "The law is color blind." How many of us have prejudices in our hearts against our fellow man simply because he is of a different color? We must vigorously attempt to rip out such prejudices once and for all; we must be willing to work and struggle—if need be—for the rights of our fellow men who happen to have been born Negroes. In many respects, this will be the great test of whether we want to practice what we preach.

We cannot love our fellow man and discriminate against him. This is an impossibility. You do not segregate or separate those whom you really love. It is as simple as that. Christ is present in the Negro as well as in the white man. Whatever we do to him, we do to Christ Himself. "Amen I say to you, as long as you did it for one of these, the least of my brethren, you did it for me" (Matt. 2, 40).

DISCUSSION QUESTIONS

1. What do we mean by the social teachings of the Church?
2. Why can this encyclical be addressed "to all men of good will"?
3. What is the rock bottom foundation on which peace is to be built?

4. What is religious freedom? Why is it a right of every man?

5. What do we mean by civil rights? Why is it so important that Catholics take part in this movement?

6. What are the responsibilities connected with man's rights?

7. What does the Pope mean when he says that society is above all a spiritual reality?

8. How can we say that all men are our brothers? Do we have any obligations toward them?

9. Why is the position of woman in modern affairs so important today?

10. What is racism? Why is it such a great evil?

11. What is discrimination? What does the Pope have to say about it?

PART 2
Relations
Between Individuals
And Public Authorities
Within One Country

As we have said, the Holy Father is building his encyclical like a house. The foundation was laid regarding the rights of the human person. This is the "rock-bottom" foundation of the encyclical. In this section, the Holy Father investigates the relations between persons and the government or what the Holy Father calls "the State."

We have already seen that the most important job of the State is to safeguard and promote the individual rights of every man in its society. In this way, each person can be assured of the greatest amount of freedom and protection possible. Through the social security system, for instance, it insures each citizen against the fear of having nothing when we become old and unable to work. By the State protecting each of its citizens through the Bill of Rights, each of these citizens has the freedom to vote, to publish, and to read books.

However, it is not the State that *gives* these freedoms to its citizens; on the contrary, we have seen that God gave each man and woman these rights when He created them. The State must simply see to it that these rights and freedoms are guarded and protected. It is this point that the Holy Father discusses in this part of his encyclical.

46. Human society can be neither well-ordered nor prosperous unless it has some people invested with legitimate authority to preserve its institutions and to devote themselves as far as is necessary to work and care for the good of all. These, however derive their authority from God, as St. Paul teaches in the words, *There exists no authority except from God* (Rom. 13, 1-6). These words of St. Paul are explained thus by St. John Chrysostom: *What are you saying? Is every ruler appointed by God? I do not say that*, he replies, *for I am not dealing now with individual rulers, but with authority itself. What I say is, that it is the divine wisdom and not mere chance, that has ordained that there should be government, that some should command and others obey.* Moreover, since God made men social by nature, and since no society *can hold together unless some one be over all, directing all to strive earnestly for the common good, every civilized community must have a ruling authority, and this authority, no less than society itself, has its source in nature, and has, consequently, God for its author* (Leo XIII, *Immortale Dei*).

The Holy Father first explains that the authority of the State and of the government is both necessary and good. Some men hold that the authority of the government is only "an evil which is necessary." This is not true. God has made us social by nature. We have seen that this means that we need each other, we depend on each other. God has not made us completely independent, but He has made us in such a way that each of us has abilities and qualities that other people need. We, in turn, need the abilities and the talents of these other people. If I build a house, for example, I must get a carpenter, a plumber. There must be factories to make nails and miners to dig the iron ore, etc. God did not intend us to live alone. I need soldiers and policemen to protect me, bakers and butchers to feed me, truck drivers and automobile manufacturers to transport my goods, etc.

So the work of the authority of the State is to see to it that everything runs smoothly and justly. It protects me from people who would charge me too much for what I buy; it repairs roads for goods to travel on; it sees to it that my food is pure and the medicines I take are healthful. The government, then, has the authority to protect the good of the country's citizens.

It is true that some governments oppress the citizens; they forbid religious freedom and free elections. But such an authority is an *abuse* and, to tell the truth, when a government acts like that, it loses its authority over its citizens. That is why we call these governments "totalitarian"; they are a form of tyranny.

Thus, the government is a service to the people. Its first duty is to serve the good of its citizens. That is why we call public officials "ministers" because they *serve* the people. However, the job of the government is not to do everything for its citizens but to help them do things themselves. When the government tries to do everything, this is called "collectivism" or "Statism" and this is a great evil. The government must regulate many activities in the state but only in order that each citizen might do things for himself more easily. We will see more of this later. If these things are true, concludes the Holy Father, then the authority of the State comes from God. As he says:

47. But authority is not to be thought of as a force lacking all control. Indeed, since it has the power to command according to right reason, authority must derive its obligatory force from the moral order, which in turn has God for its first source and final end. Wherefore Our Predecessor of happy memory, Pius XII, said: *That same absolute order of beings and their ends which presents man as an autonomous person, that is, as the subject of inviolable duties and rights, and as at once the basis of society and the purpose for which it exists, also includes the State as a necessary society invested with the authority without which it could not come into being or live . . .* (Cf. Radio Broadcast, Christmas Eve, 1944).

Thus, if the authority does anything that is against the law of God by denying men their rights and freedoms, it loses all claim to authority. It is no longer what we call a "legitimate authority" but a tyranny. Each citizen should have equal protection of the laws regardless of race, color or creed. As it says in the *Declaration of Independence*:

We hold these truths to be self evident, that all men are created equal, that they are en-

dowed by their Creator with certain inalienable rights, that among these are life,
liberty and the pursuit of happiness. That
to secure these rights, governments are insti-
tuted among men, deriving their just powers
from the consent of the governed, that whenever any form of government becomes destructive of these ends, it is the right of the
people to alter or abolish it.

The Holy Father says the same thing:

51. Since the right to command is required by the
moral order and has its source in God, it follows
that, if civil authorities legislate for or allow anything that is contrary to that order and therefore
contrary to the will of God, neither the laws made
nor the authorizations granted can be binding on
the consciences of the citizens, since *we must obey
God rather than men* (Acts 5, 29). Otherwise, authority breaks down completely and results in
shameful abuse.

The Holy Father certainly does not mean that
authority comes directly from God, that the people do not have a right to choose their own government. Authority comes from God in this
sense, that as long as the government protects and
promotes the rights and freedoms of each of its
citizens, it is just and pleasing to God. When it
does not do so, it is an unjust government and
cannot be pleasing to God because it acts immorally. The people, however, have a right to choose
those who will represent them and pass laws for
them. They do this at specified times (election

day) by "voting." This is what we call a truly democratic way of life which the Pope praises when he says explicitly:

52. It must not be concluded, however, because authority comes from God, that therefore men have no right to choose those who are to rule the State, to decide the form of government, and to determine both the way in which authority is to be exercised and its limits. It is thus clear that the doctrine which We have set forth is fully consonant with any truly democratic regime.

Next, the Pope discusses what he means by the "common good." Simply stated, it means the welfare of all the citizens. In other words, the job of the government is to see to it that the good of all of its citizens is promoted, not just the good of a few individuals. When the government passes laws for only a few, say the rich, then the majority of the people suffers. This is an immoral action on the part of the government because the rich, having a lot of money, can influence government officials while the poor have no one to speak for them. The government acts immorally because it does not act for the good of all of its citizens. But what are the conditions necessary for the common good? They are two and the Holy Father lists them both.

55. Assuredly, the ethnic characteristics of the various human groups are to be respected as constituent elements of the common good, but these values and characteristics by no means exhaust the content of

the common good. For the common good is intimately bound up with human nature. It can never exist fully and completely unless, its intimate nature and realization being what they are, the human person is taken into account.

The world is composed of many nations and of many races. God has created each and since this is so, each of them has qualities and richness that the others do not. Thus, as we have said, we must work together in order to share what we have. We are dependent on each other and in today's world, no nation, no race, can exist by itself.

The Holy Father says that the different characteristics (qualities) that each race and nation has must be safeguarded and promoted by other people and nations. This is not strange since the richness of the whole human family comes from the individual richness of each of the members of that family. We are all equal insofar as we are men created by God and destined for eternal life; we are all unequal in the amount of talent that God has given to each of us.

The common good requires that we protect both this equality and the different riches that each race, each nation and each individual possesses. The State must do all in its power to do likewise through its laws and regulations. For example, where did the great riches of the U.S. come from? They came from the many different races of people who came here from all over the world: black, white, yellow; Italians, Germans, Japanese, Irish, etc. Each of these races were not destroyed in the melting pot but rather each made its contribution to the common good.

The Pope continues with the second characteristic:

56. In the second place, the very nature of the common good requires that all members of the political community be entitled to share in it, although in different ways according to each one's tasks, merits and circumstances. For this reason, every civil authority must take pains to promote the common good of all, without preference for any single citizen or civic group. As Our Predecessor of immortal memory, Leo XIII, has said: *The civil power must not serve the advantage of any one individual, or of some few persons, inasmuch as it was established for the common good of all (Immortale Dei)*. Considerations of justice and equity, however, can at times demand that those involved in civil government give more attention to the less fortunate members of the community, since they are less able to defend their rights and to assert their legitimate claims.

Since each man and woman has contributed something to the common good of all of the citizens—no matter how small—each has a right to share in the good that society produces. The concept should be: "Each one should give of his talents, etc., according to his abilities and each one should receive what he needs according to the degree of his need." I have a right to share in social security, sick benefits, old age pensions, art shows, education, political life because I have something to give other men with whom I live.

But each of us will share in these goods of society in various ways. We share according to our *abilities*. For instance, if I have no appreciation for art, I can't very well enjoy an art show. We share also according to our *merit*, for instance, if one man has worked harder at a job (all other things being equal) he will be entitled to more than the man who does not work so hard. The important thing to remember is that all of the citizens must share, at least to some degree, in the goods and life of the society in which they live. Otherwise, the common good is not fulfilled and there is an injustice committed in society.

It can happen that at times the government must give special consideration to those who have nothing or at least very little. This is so because the poor usually have no defenders. In America where money plays a role of primary importance, who wants to promote and protect the cause of the poor (e.g. aged, disabled, unemployed, etc.)? There are, unfortunately, very few in our society who are willing to do this. Therefore, the government, as we have said, must take care of the good of all the citizens and must see to it that they are helped by promoting their welfare. They must not be neglected and so the government is quite correct in passing such legislation as old age insurance and medical care for the aged.

58. These principles are definitely implied in what was stated in Our Encyclical, *Mater et Magistra,* where We emphasized that the common good of all *embraces the sum total of those conditions of*

*social living whereby men are enabled to achieve
their own integral perfection more fully and more
easily (Mater et Magistra).*
59. Men, however, composed as they are of bodies
and immortal souls, can never in this mortal life
succeed in satisfying all their needs or in attaining
perfect happiness. Therefore all efforts made to
promote the common good, far from endangering
the eternal salvation of men, ought rather to serve
to promote it.

Here in paragraph 58 the Holy Father gives, in
summary form, a definition of the common good,
those conditions by which many can achieve
their total perfection on this earth; and immedi-
ately the Holy Father adds paragraph 59 to show
exactly what he means by this type of perfection.
God created man as both a body and a soul. A
man's body is just as much a part of God's creation as his soul and, consequently, he must take
care of it as God wills him to do. Therefore,
man's perfection on this earth is both material
and spiritual.

It is material because man needs many material things to stay alive—food, shelter, security,
etc., for himself and his family. This is important because Christianity must worry about these
things as well. The spiritual is also part of man's
perfection because man has a soul as well. Man
has spiritual needs such as art, education, culture,
religion. The State—and all citizens within each
State—must see to it that conditions are present
so that each man and woman may enjoy the best
possible opportunities to develop these needs.

There could, at this point, be an objection to this thought of the Holy Father. Does not a working for man's good here on this earth take his attention away from heaven and the next world? Not at all, says the Pope; and why not? For the simple reason that, first, it is God's will that man develop himself as fully as possible. That is why God put all the beautiful material and spiritual things on this earth. Secondly, without a certain amount of development and perfection here on earth, man cannot worship God properly. A starving man can, only with the greatest difficulty, think of God. Therefore, this "well being" of man on earth is, as it were, a preparation for the next world and heaven.

60. It is agreed that in our time the common good is chiefly guaranteed when personal rights and duties are maintained. The chief concern of civil authorities must therefore be to ensure that these rights are acknowledged, respected, co-ordinated with other rights, defended and promoted, so that in this way each one may more easily carry out his duties. For *to safeguard the inviolable rights of the human person, and to facilitate the fulfillment of his duties, should be the essential office of every public authority* (Pius XII, Radio Broadcast, June 1, 1941).
61. This means that, if any government does not acknowledge the rights of man or violates them it not only fails in its duty, but its orders completely lack juridical force.

It is important to note how often the Holy Father comes back to the same theme: The common good is promoted above all when the State and the citizens of the country promote the human and civil rights of each of its citizens. And it is not only in Communistic countries that this is not done. Right here in the United States, how many times are Negroes denied their rights as citizens? Many, many times. We have only to read the newspapers to see for ourselves. If this be so, how is it possible that in our society, such a thing as a Civil Rights bill has had so much trouble in our Congress? Because both as Americans and as Christians, we have not and are not now willing to practice what we preach. This is a great tragedy when we portray ourselves to the world as being the great defenders of democracy. And we practice it so little right in our own back yard. Here is a job for us all.

The Holy Father does not tell us *how* to go about doing this valuable work. He simply tells us our duties and expects us to find the best way to solve the problem. This is so throughout the encyclical. After all, the Holy Father is addressing all the world, not just the United States. Therefore, we must find our own solutions to the problems which face us today.

63. It is also demanded by the common good that civil authorities should make earnest efforts to bring about a situation in which individual citizens can easily exercise their rights and fulfill their duties as well. For experience has taught us that, unless these authorities take suitable action with regard to economic, political and cultural matters, inequalities between the citizens tend to become more and more

widespread, especially in the modern world, and as a result, a man's rights and duties in some way lack effectiveness.

The Pope expects the government to take vigorous action whenever it is demanded. When is it called for? Whenever the weaker people of the community are in danger. For instance, if something is not done to the economy to make it pick up, there will be many unemployed who will have no power to do anything about it. The government through such measures as unemployment insurance and tax cuts can remedy the situation. Again, when some companies become so large that they can fix prices at whatever level they please, the small businessman is in danger of losing his business and he can do nothing about it. Therefore, the government must step in with anti-trust acts and force the large companies to be just in their dealings and prices. It is along these lines that our government was thinking when it passed the large tax cut in February, 1964. By cutting taxes, consumers will have more money in order to stimulate the economy.

We must also mention here, President Johnson's "War on Poverty." There are some 35 million Americans who either are unable or incapable of sharing the growing prosperity of America. They are truly poor. They include the aged, unemployed in depressed areas. Negroes and other minority groups, migrant workers, etc. The government's program to retrain them when possible, to provide skills and housing and in general to increase their purchasing power is certainly a great step in the right direction. We have neglected them too long and our Christian consciences have forgotten them too long in our quest for "the good life." After all, was it not our Lord Himself who told us that He is identified with them in a special way? Is not such a program profoundly Christian?

All these things are specially true in the modern world because everything has become so complicated that the government must constantly keep its eye on things so no one gets cheated or suffers unjustly. Think, for instance, how complicated it is to make an airplane: metals from all over the world, many technicians and highly trained personnel, precision instruments, etc., are needed. Our modern life has become very complex and it is easy for some or even many individuals to suffer unjustly in such a situation.

Next, the Pope goes on to investigate what form the government should take in this complicated modern world. He says:

68. In determining the structure and operation of government which a State is to have, great weight has to be given to the historical background and circumstances of the individual peoples, circumstances which will vary at different times and in different places. We consider, however, that it is in keeping with the innate demands of human nature that the State should take a form which embodies the threefold division of powers corresponding to the three principal functions of public authority. In that type of State, not only the official functions of government

but also the mutual relations between citizens and public officials are set down according to law. This in itself affords protection to the citizens both in the enjoyment of their rights and in the fulfillment of their duties.

A true democracy (as we saw earlier) is really a very difficult type of government to form. Why? Because the people must be educated at least to a certain degree in order to understand the issues and to have the ability to vote correctly and choose their representatives wisely. This means a whole network of education, schools of all kinds, and money with which to build them. Many countries of the world are not yet adequately developed in this way, so democracy has a much more difficult time surviving in those places. Therefore, says the Pope, we cannot just say "One form of democracy for everybody" because conditions are different throughout the world (par. 67-68).

But what the Holy Father does want is that the duties of government be divided into three main sections: the legislative which makes the laws; the executive which enforces the laws; and the judiciary which interprets the laws. This is exactly as we have it in this country where we have the Congress, the President, and the Supreme Court. Each acts as a check and balance on the other so that neither of the three can gain complete control of the country. This is very wise for it is never good to entrust the government to either one man or one group of men. If the Congress makes an unjust law, or a law which is not good for the citizens, the President can veto the bill and finally, if need be, the Supreme Court can declare it unconstitutional, thus, the law becomes invalid. This democratic way of life is praised by the Holy Father.

In short, what the Holy Father is praising in a democracy is that government gets its "just powers from the consent of the governed" (*Declaration of Independence*). This government "of the people, by the people and for the people" is brought about by free discussion and debate about what is best for the people. It must not be the result of force or violence by one man or a group of men (tyranny). Each citizen is equal before the law from the President down to the most humble worker. This is what the Pope means when he says:

... Moreover, executive authorities must co-ordinate the activities of society with discretion, with a full knowledge of the law and after a careful consideration of circumstances, and the courts must administer justice impartially and without being influenced by favoritism or pressure. The good order of society also demands that individual citizens and intermediate organizations should be effectively protected by law whenever they have rights to be exercised or obligations to be fulfilled. This protection should be granted to citizens both in their dealings with each other and in their relations with government agencies.

In this way, injustices will be avoided and each

citizen will have the equal protection of all the laws for himself and his family.

But the Holy Father goes even further when he says:

75. Accordingly, it follows that in our day, where there is question of organizing political communities juridically, it is required first of all that there be written in concise and limpid phraseology, a charter of fundamental human rights, and that this be inserted in the basic law of the State.

76. Secondly, it is required that the Constitution of each political community be formulated in proper legal terminology, and that there be defined therein the manner in which the State authorities are to be designated, how their mutual relations are to be regulated, what are to be their spheres of competence, and finally, the forms and systems they are obliged to follow in the performance of their office.

77. Finally, it is required that the relations between the government and the citizens be set forth in detail in terms of rights and duties, and that it be distinctly decreed that a major task of the government is that of recognizing, respecting, reconciling, protecting and promoting the rights and duties of citizens.

The wisdom of the Holy Father is very evident in these three paragraphs. Many things must be written down in order to ensure that all will be carried out correctly. We in this country are very fortunate. We have our rights and freedoms written down in documents that we call our Constitution, the Bill of Rights, and the Declaration of Independence. In them we can see clearly what the Holy Father means when he says that the rights of the citizens be "written in concise and limpid phraseology" for all to see and study. In this way, we have written down what we can do and cannot do; what the government can do and what it cannot do.

Secondly, the manner of electing public officials to the government must also be clearly outlined in this constitution. This will prevent someone who has not been duly elected by the people from taking over the government. Men who wish to have a position in the government must follow the manner which the constitution establishes for that purpose. This assures order in the government and prevents corrupt men from fooling the citizens.

And finally, the duties between government and its citizens must also be clearly stated in the constitution. History shows that when this is not done, much mistreatment can be performed by the State which forces its citizens to do things that it has no right to force them to do. If the government does so, the citizen should be able then to appeal to the courts which will declare the law unconstitutional. In this way, the citizen has the greatest protection of his rights.

78. It is of course impossible to accept the theory which professes to find the original and unique source of civic rights and duties, of the binding force of the Constitution, and of a government's right to command, in the mere will of human beings, individually or collectively.

In America we sometimes get the impression that everything is good or bad because the majority of the people say it is or say that it is not. In many cases, we determine that we are going to do something by means of the "majority rule." But this is not right when it becomes necessary to explain the origin of the rights of men. Men (or government) cannot give other men their rights; only God can do this because only God has created man. Each man and woman has rights because he or she was so created by God and the "majority" of the people can only recognize this fact. It cannot grant or take them away. The right of the government to command and the right of citizens to respect for their rights come from God alone, and not from the will of most of the people.

To sum up this section, laws are for the protection of the rights of man and the tendency is to put these rights down in black and white. The rights of citizens are thereby better secured. No one is above all law—not even the government. The law is for everyone and everyone must respect it.

The duty of the State is to promote the common good of all of its citizens, protecting and ensuring the rights of all of the citizens. Without this authority, there would be confusion and injustice in society. In this sense, the State's authority comes from God because it is necessary for man's material and spiritual good. We each have our share to do by contributing our talents and abilities for the good of all. The government, in its turn, has the serious obligation of protecting and promoting the rights of all of its citizens. The State is then a means to an end; it is a service of the social life of the whole community. The goal of the human community is liberty which is achieved through justice, respecting the truth of the moral law and the sacredness of the rights of man.

DISCUSSION QUESTIONS

1. Why is authority necessary in every State?
2. What do we mean when we say that all authority is from God?
3. What is the principal duty and task of the State?
4. What documents in American history do we have which show what the Holy Father means when he says that the State must protect the rights of its citizens?
5. When are the laws of the State "binding in conscience" on its citizens? When are they not?
6. What do we mean by democratic government? Does the Pope approve of this type of government?
7. What is the common good? What are its parts?
8. Why is the Church worried about a man's body as well as his soul?
9. Give and explain the three divisions of government which the Pope praises in his encyclical.
10. Should the majority always rule? Explain.

PART 3
Relations
Between States

IN THIS SECTION, the Holy Father is going to treat the relationship between countries. The Pope says that each country has a right to exist and to be independent of all other countries in the world. This automatically rules out any notion that one country or one people is better than another. This is what we call *racism* and the Holy Father condemns it with all of his power. Why is this so? Because nations are all composed of individual human beings who have all been created equal by God.

Thus, in this section as in the previous two, the most fundamental thing to remember is the rights of each and every human person.

The relationship between two countries is governed by "international law." This obliges all men to respect the human person and the rights of all men. If this is not respected between nations, then we are left with the "law of the jungle" which rules men, who, in this case, are not men at all, but mere beasts looking for survival at the price of their adversary. This is just the opposite of what the Pope has in mind when he explains this relationship. He now goes on to develop what this relationship ought to be.

80. Our Predecessors have constantly maintained,

and We join them in reasserting, that political communities are reciprocally subjects of rights and duties. This means that their relationships also must be harmonized in truth, in justice, in a working solidarity, in liberty. For the same natural law, which governs relations between individual human beings, must also regulate the relations of political communities with one another.

In the first section of his encyclical, the Holy Father has already explained what he means by this "natural law." It means basically, the respect of the human person along with his rights and freedoms. This is absolutely necessary if there is to be any peace between one nation and another. Thus nations as well as individuals are ruled by the *moral law,* that is to say, they are responsible to God for their actions. If they act morally, then nations are pleasing to God; if they do not, then they are not doing God's will. Nations cannot be ruled by force. Just because one nation is bigger or more powerful than another does not mean that it can do anything it wishes with nations that are smaller and weaker. Unfortunately, this has been the case in human history. But it only means that nations have acted immorally or have not acted according to God's law or His will.

Today, it is no longer possible to build the relations between nations on power and force, because now man has developed so much power that he is capable of destroying himself and the earth as well. There remains only one alternative to total destruction and ruin: the order of respect and promotion of the human rights of man. The will of each country must be ruled not just by power, or self-interest; it must seriously take into consideration the rights of others, for they have just as much right to independence and growth as any other nation.

81. This will be readily understood when one reflects that the individual representatives of political communities cannot put aside their personal dignity while they are acting in the name and interest of their countries; and that they cannot therefore violate the very law of nature by which they are bound, which is itself the moral law.

82. It would be absurd, moreover, even to imagine that men could surrender their own human attributes, or be compelled to do so, by the very fact of their appointment to public office. Rather, they have been given that noble assignment precisely because the wealth of their human endowments has earned them their reputation as outstanding members of the body politic.

There are some who say that the man of public office in the government has a "double standard" of conduct for his actions. He must, in other words, act one way when he is a private citizen and quite another when he is a public official. This is not correct, says the Pope. Each man and woman must act in strict conformity to his moral and religious principles whenever he acts either as a private citizen or as a public official. Why is this? For the simple reason that every person must endeavor to please God and obey His will in everything he does, whatever that might be. For instance, God expects our President always to act according to his conscience, according to his moral and religious principles in or out of public office. To say the opposite, would mean that we could please God and not please Him at one and the same time. This is obviously an absurdity. Machiavelli, a political writer of Florence, who lived in the 15th-16th centuries wrote the following advice for the ruler of his country: "Do not keep faith when by so doing it would be against your interest." This statement is false and unchristian and would terminate any peace between countries. There is an authority above the State and above each ruler of the State: it is the moral order of God which rules both the lives of men and of nations. No State, no government, is supreme; it must respect the existence and the rights of other countries. As the *Universal Declaration of Human Rights* says: "The recognition of the dignity inherent in all members of the human family and of their equal and inalienable rights, constitutes the foundation of liberty, justice and peace in the world."

Having discussed the moral foundation which makes just the relationship between states, the Pope now goes on to give these rules in particular. The first rule is that of truth without which only lies and deception will prevail:

86. First among the rules governing relations between political communities is that of truth. But truth requires the elimination of every trace of racism, and the consequent recognition of the principle that all States are by nature equal in dignity.

Each of them accordingly is vested with the right to existence, to self-development, to the means necessary to its attainment, and to be the one primarily responsible for this self-development. Add to that the right of each to its good name, and to the respect which is its due.

We have already seen what racism means. The Pope says that this is against the law of God who has created all nations equal as well as all men. When some men become richer or stronger than other men, they often think themselves *better* than the other men. This is simply not true. Just because a man (or a nation, which is composed of individual men) is bigger, or richer or more powerful than other men, does not make him one bit better than other men. Just because the United States is bigger and stronger than, for instance, Haiti, does not make the United States better. By no means. In our own country, because of its earlier tradition of Negro slavery, the white man sometimes considers himself better than the black man. This is simply not true since God created both black and white equal in dignity.

In addition each nation has not only the right to exist but also the right to develop itself. How is this? When God created both men and nations, he gave them all very special qualities, talents and abilities. Since this is so, these men and nations have a right given them by God to develop and perfect what God has given them. For any nation to attempt to make use of another country for its own profit is a great injustice. Often this is what we call colonialism. It was practiced by the European nations for hundreds of years in America, Africa and Asia: it is practiced today by the Soviet Union in Eastern Europe. The Pope condemns all forms of colonialism as being against God's moral law. Thus the Holy Father insists again:

87. Very often, experience has taught us, individuals will be found to differ considerably, in knowledge, virtue, talent and wealth. Yet these inequalities must never be held to excuse any man's attempt to lord it over his neighbors unjustly. They constitute rather a source of greater responsibility in the contribution which each and everyone must make toward mutual improvement.

Some nations are more developed than other nations, but this is no reason for them to be superior. On the contrary, the nation that is more economically developed has a greater responsibility to help the nations that are not so well off. Therefore, the United States has a moral obligation to help the underdeveloped countries of the world for the simple reason that God has blessed the United States with more. This is true charity for our brothers. Greater talents mean greater responsibility to the less fortunate. Thus the Holy Father continues:

88. Similarly, some nations may well have reached different levels of culture, civilization or economic development. Neither is that a sufficient reason for some to take unjust advantage of their superiority

over others; rather should they see in it an added motive for more serious commitment to the common cause of social progress.

The Pope simply repeats what he has been saying to the more developed countries of the world. The above paragraph most certainly refers to the United States in a particular way. And so the Pope concludes:

89. It is not true that some human beings are by nature superior, and others inferior. All men are equal in their natural dignity. Consequently there are no political communities that are superior by nature and none that are inferior by nature. All political communities are of equal natural dignity, since they are bodies whose membership is made up of these same human beings. Nor must it be forgotten, in this connection, that peoples can be highly sensitive, and with good reason, in matters touching their dignity and honor.

Since all men (and therefore nations) are created equal, their human dignity excludes all forms of racism. There can be no "superior race" in this world. Each country and community has its special gifts given to it by God. They are *different* but they are not *superior*. The Holy Father continuously brings us back to the rock-bottom foundation of any peace among nations: the rights, freedoms, and dignity of man. Concluding this discussion of truth as the first rule which must govern the relationship between countries, the Pope states:

90. Truth further demands that the various media

of social communications made available by modern progress, which enable the nations to know each other better, be used with serene objectivity. That need not, of course, rule out any legitimate emphasis on the positive aspects of their way of life. But methods of information which fall short of the truth, and by the same token impair the reputation of this people or that, must be discarded.

The Holy Father says that each nation has the right to be correctly informed about all other nations. If two people are going to work together, they must know each other well or else they will be suspicious of each other. If there is suspicion, then there is distrust and there can be very little cooperation between them. As a matter of fact, sooner or later, they will develop a hatred of each other and finally come to blows. So too with nations. Some nations are always telling other nations lies. In what we have termed the totalitarian state, the leaders must confuse and lie to the citizens to keep them from knowing the real situation in their countries. This is commonly called *propaganda*. Nations, says the Pope, have the obligation of always telling the truth to each other. We hear, for example, how terrible the Communist take-over in Cuba was and still is today; this is true, but what is not known usually are the reasons for this take-over. Little is known, for example, about the terrible enslavement of the Cuban people by their former dictators which was at least one of the primary causes of that island's eventual inclusion in the Communist sphere. We must attempt to understand the truth of the world situation, not just what one country has to say about it. We have the right to know and nations have the obligation to inform us. Equally misleading, on the other hand, is the terrible image spread in other countries by United States movies and television of the "American way of life" portraying violence, sex, and materialism. This is not the true picture of the United States. As President Johnson said at the opening of the World's Fair (1964), we have our problems in this country with regard to the race problem but we are trying our best to overcome them (cf. Civil Rights Bill). The Soviet press only insists on the dark aspect of the problem without pointing out our positive achievements. This is unfair as well as a distortion. Other nations have a right to know what we really stand for, not what Hollywood says we are: we can say that the true picture of the American way of life is the sacred position of the individual and his dignity. This is the important thing in the American way of life; other nations have a right to know that.

From truth, the first rule governing the relations between nations, the Pope proceeds to justice, the second rule:

93. Not only can it happen, but it actually does happen that the advantages and conveniences which nations strive to acquire for themselves become objects of contention; nevertheless, the resulting disagreements must be settled, not by arms, nor by deceit or trickery, but rather in the only manner which is worthy of the dignity of man, i.e., by a mutual assess-

ment of the reasons on both sides of the dispute, by a mature and objective investigation of the situation, and by an equitable reconciliation of differences of opinion.

Many times between nations there is bound to be some conflict of economic interests. For instance, certain fishing areas disputed by Japanese and Alaskan fishermen have led to a conflict of interests between Japan and the United States. This can be equally true of trade between nations. What is to be done? In the past, many nations have gone to war with each other to solve these problems. But this really solves nothing. The only thing it proves is who is stronger, not who is right. The Holy Father says that this is not the just way to settle differences between individual nations. Men of good will must attempt to negotiate, that is, try to see all sides of the problem and come to a solution that will be just and agreeable to all. In this manner, men can rule better in peace than in war.

While truth and justice are very important in the relations between nations, it is not enough. The fact is that all men are brothers (created by God) and that, therefore, all nations should care for each other, treating each other as brothers. They have the obligation to aid each other, to help each other develop in all possible ways. This is what the Holy Father is going to develop now and this is what he means when he says "active solidarity."

98. Because relations between States must be regu-

lated by the norms of truth and justice, they should also derive great benefits from active solidarity, through mutual cooperation on various levels, such as, in our own times, has already taken place with laudable results in the economic, social, political, educational, health and sport spheres. We must remember that, of its very nature, civil authority exists, not to confine its people within the boundaries of their nation, but rather to protect, above all else, the common good of that particular civil society, which certainly cannot be divorced from the common good of the entire human family.

In our day and age, nations are becoming more and more dependent on each other from every point of view. No nation, for example, can be self-sufficient in the trade of goods. This is simply impossible today. It is easily understood when we realize how wretched and poor the majority of the people on earth really are. Over two-thirds of the people on earth go to bed hungry every night while in other nations — such as in the United States—we actually can waste food. Thus, today's world is divided into the "have nations" (17% of the world's population) and the "have-not nations" (about 80% of the world's population). If, therefore, nations are true brothers created by God, can there be any doubt in anyone's mind that the former must come to the aid of the latter? In another one of Pope John's encyclicals, he calls this obligation one of justice, that is, one which the rich nations must perform because God wants it so. The peoples of the earth must join forces to develop and help the less fortunate, the hungry, the sick and those who have nothing in this world. Therefore, the Holy Father appeals:

99. This entails not only that civil societies should pursue their particular interests without hurting others, but also that they should join forces and plans whenever the efforts of an individual government cannot achieve its desired goals . . .

But the Pope does not stop at just economic or material goods. These are important but man possesses more than just economic goods. To live a really full life, man must live a spiritual, artistic, and cultural life as well. Each nation, each group, has a particular gift from God in each of these fields. The Pope encourages them to develop these gifts. Why? So that all of mankind will be enriched. That is why we have such projects as student exchange programs to profit from the riches of others and so that they can profit from our contributions. As the Holy Father explains:

100. Furthermore, the universal common good requires that in every nation friendly relations be fostered in all fields between the citizens and their intermediate societies. There are groupings of people of more or less different ethnic backgrounds. However, the elements which characterize an ethnic group must not be transformed into a watertight compartment in which human beings are prevented from communicating with their fellow men belonging to different ethnic groups. That would contrast with our contemporary situation, in which the distances separating peoples have been almost wiped out. Nor can one overlook the fact that, even though human beings differ from one another by virtue of their eth-

nic peculiarities, they all possess certain essential common elements of considerable importance, whereby they can progressively develop and perfect themselves, especially in the realm of spiritual values. They have the right and duty therefore to live in communion with one another.

It is very clear that the Pope does not fear the goods of this earth or man's gifts from God. On the contrary, he encourages man to develop these gifts and abilities. What is more, he says that it is the will of God that man do so as much and as best he can.

Man, says the Holy Scripture, has been put on this earth as God's lieutenant. He is to continue God's work of creation, in a sense, by developing all the resources and materials which God created at the beginning of time. Man must view his work—whatever it be—as a gift of God for the betterment of his fellow man in love. As Pope John himself put it so well in *Mater et Magistra*:

> For it is indeed clear that the Church has always taught and continues to teach that advances in science and technology and the prosperity resulting therefrom, are truly to be counted as good things and regarded as signs of the progress of civilization (par. 246).

And again in that same encyclical, he says:

> . . . It must be added that when one is motivated by Christian charity, he cannot but love others, and regard the needs, sufferings

and joys of others as his own. His work, wherever it be, is constant, adaptable, humane, and has concern for the needs of others . . . (par. 257).

This is indeed a beautiful Christian picture of human work and endeavor on this earth given to us by God.

The great vision of heaven and earth that Pope John has is truly remarkable. All is God's creation given to men and they have the obligation of developing that creation according to God's plans. And the Pope is happy to bless man's accomplishments. For the first time in history, man, through the abilities given him by God, can control disease and hunger everywhere on the face of the earth. He need no longer fear floods and droughts as much as in the past. These goods have been given to man not just for the use of one group of people or one nation but for all nations and for all men. The whole human race is one great family because it was created by God. They are brothers and for this reason, they must share everything with each other. They must not hold back like Cain who said: "Am I my brother's keeper?" The answer should have been, yes, you are your brother's keeper just as we are all our brothers' keepers.

It must also be remembered, however, that man's progress in science and industry can backfire. That is, it can be used for war and destruction. For example, science has produced nuclear energy which can be used for great good as a source of mankind's advance or it can also be used in nuclear bombs to destroy and kill mankind. Therefore, we must be careful to say with the Holy Father that all of these advances of science are good only if they are used according to God's will. And what is this will of God? This is exactly what the Holy Father has been explaining when he says that men must be ruled by the *moral law,* in truth and justice and love. Without these virtues, without these guidelines, man is headed toward his own destruction.

After this discussion of the need for "active solidarity" among men, the Holy Father goes on to examine some of the great problems that require the effort and cooperation of the whole world to solve. The first of these is the problem of overpopulation.

101. As everybody knows, there are countries with an abundance of arable land and a scarcity of manpower, while in other countries there is no proportion between natural resources and the capital available. This demands that peoples should set up relationships of mutual collaboration, facilitating the circulation from one to the other of goods, capital, and manpower.

Lately, some men have been saying that the world has too many people in it and that soon there will not be enough food and land for everyone. This is what we call the problem of "overpopulation," that the Pope discusses.

First of all, is there really such a problem ? We can say that it does exist in certain parts of the world. In certain regions, there is not enough production of economic goods for everyone and it is precisely in those countries where the population is getting larger continually. Areas such as Latin America, India, and Egypt have this problem. Is there any solution to it? Yes, and the Pope explains.

One major reason why there isn't enough food and goods is because of the poor and backward methods used in these countries for farming and raising crops. They need to learn modern farming, the use of fertilizers, etc., to get a better crop from the land. A UN organization entitled FAO (Food and Agricultural Organization) is doing a great deal in this field to bring this about.

Another solution and aid is *immigration*. This occurs when people of an overcrowded area move to other areas where there are few people. The Holy Father encourages the various nations (who can) to open up their countries to people of poorer nations, giving them a new home and work to do. In this way, a better distribution of the people of the world could be obtained.

Therefore, the Pope is optimistic for the future. He does not say that there is no problem. Although the problem of rapid population growth unhappily exists he says that man has the ability and the intelligence to find solutions to this problem. He is not a pessimist seeing the world about to be overcome with too many mouths to feed.

Yet, overpopulation is only one of the many

problems that face us today. The problem of political refugees presents another serious difficulty requiring the cooperation of all nations.

103. The sentiment of universal fatherhood which the Lord has placed in Our heart makes Us feel profound sadness in considering the phenomenon of political refugees: a phenomenon which has assumed large proportions and which always hides numberless and acute sufferings.

104. Such expatriations show that there are some political regimes which do not guarantee for individual citizens a sufficient sphere of freedom within which they can lead a life worthy of man. In fact, under those regimes even the very right to freedom is either called into question or openly denied. This undoubtedly is a radical inversion of the order of human society, because the reason for the existence of public authority is to promote the common good, a fundamental element of which is to recognize freedom and to safeguard it.

There are some countries that oppress their citizens to such a degree, denying them their fundamental rights and liberties, that their sole hope is for escape from such oppression. This results in political refugees, that is, those who have fled their native lands because they were denied their liberty and freedom. The people who have fled East Germany, Cuban refugees, Hungarian freedom fighters and Chinese families in Hong Kong have all escaped from the terrible oppression of communism. Under communism these people really had no rights since it is the State that "grants" rights to its citizens and all are then the subjects of the all powerful State.

By such a doctrine, man becomes only a cog in a machine, no different from an animal. We have seen time and time again that the Holy Father holds just the opposite view. The State exists for man and not man for the State. We must never forget this. That is why communism, as a doctrine and as a teaching, can never be reconciled with the teachings of Christ (or of the Church that teaches in the name of Christ).

In view of this denial of human freedom and rights in the communistic as well as other totalitarian States, the Holy Father encourages the free nations of the world to welcome these political refugees receiving them as full citizens so that they might live in "a sphere (area) of freedom within which their souls are allowed to breathe humanly." Catholics have done much to obey the wishes of the Holy Father. The NCWC in Washington, D.C. is always finding homes and jobs for these people. A Belgian Dominican priest, Father Domenic Pire, has received the Nobel Peace Prize for building whole villages and cities in Europe for the refugees of both World War II and of communistic countries. We need many more Father Pires.

The last problem which faces individual countries is perhaps the most serious of all—the problem of disarmament, or the effort to reduce the quantity of arms in the world. It is the most serious because it is a threat to the survival of man. The Holy Father now discusses this great problem.

109. On the other hand, it is with deep sorrow that We note the enormous stocks of armaments that have been and still are being made in more economically developed countries, with a vast outlay of intellectual and economic resources. And so it happens that, while the people of these countries are loaded with heavy burdens, other countries as a result are deprived of the collaboration they need in order to make economic and social progress.

110. The production of arms is allegedly justified on the grounds that in present-day conditions peace cannot be preserved without an equal balance of armaments. And so, if one country increases its armaments, others feel the need to do the same; and if one country is equipped with nuclear weapons, other countries must produce their own, equally destructive.

111. Consequently, people live in constant fear lest the storm that every moment threatens should break upon them with dreadful violence. And with good reason, for the arms of war are ready at hand. Even though it is difficult to believe that anyone would deliberately take the responsibility for the appalling destruction and sorrow that war would bring in its train, it cannot be denied that the conflagration may be set off by some unexpected and obscure event. And one must bear in mind that, even though the monstrous power of modern weapons acts as a deterrent, it is to be feared that the mere continuance of nuclear tests, undertaken with war in mind, will prove a serious hazard for life on earth.

112. Justice, then, right reason and humanity urgently demand that the arms race should cease; that the stockpiles which exist in various countries should be reduced equally and simultaneously by the parties concerned; that nuclear weapons should be banned; and that a general agreement should eventually be reached about progressive disarma-

ment and an effective method of control. In the words of Pius XII, Our Predecessor of happy memory: *The calamity of a world war, with the economic and social ruin and the moral excesses and dissolution that accompany it, must not be permitted to envelop the human race for a third time* (Cf. Radio Broadcast, Christmas Eve, 1941).

The Pope makes a moving appeal to all of the world's nations—particularly to those who have the most destructive arms at hand—to seriously consider reducing the number of these arms. What reasons does he give? First, he says, the danger is very great for the survival of the human race. Each side tries to outstrip and outnumber the other in powerful weapons. Each side claims that it must do so because the other side is doing the same thing. Thus, if one has a nuclear bomb of 100 megatons, the other claims that it too must develop a similar one for defense purposes. To make the problem more difficult, many nations are beginning to develop these weapons and soon at least ten nations will have them. Anything can happen. Even an accident can start a war that could obliterate man from the face of the earth. It's like playing with matches in a dynamite factory. Even if you don't mean it, an accident could blow the whole place sky high. Distrusting each other, the nations build bigger and bigger weapons of nuclear energy — then through some accident, the whole world is blown sky high. The Holy Father urges the nations, through pacts and mutual agreements, to reduce these weapons before it is too late. A great step in this direction was taken, for instance, when Russia and the United States signed the nuclear treaty of October, 1963. Both sides agreed not to test nuclear bombs in the air.

Another complaint against armaments is the tremendous cost of these weapons. Last year, the United States military budget was over fifty billion dollars! That is enough money to develop all of the world's underdeveloped countries. It is indeed unfortunate that we must spend so much money on arms and weapons when two-thirds of the world's people go to bed hungry every night.

The Holy Father, for these reasons, calls on the nations of the world to reduce their arms thereby lessening the danger of a nuclear war. But, he adds, there must be *effective controls*. This has proved an obstacle because some nations (Russia) have refused to allow any control. But without controls, someone could always cheat and the danger remains. How are these controls to be established? The Holy Father does not answer this question here but will give it in the next part of his encyclical when he discusses the U.N. Still men must continue to try to negotiate disarmament. It is the only hope of the human race's survival. Its effects will be felt by all peoples in all nations. We must do everything in our power to bring this about. Christ wants peace in the world, not hate and death. It is the very serious obligation of each and every Catholic to work for peace in any way that he can. Thus, concludes the Holy Father:

116. And finally, it is an objective which will be a fruitful source of many benefits, for its advantages will be felt everywhere, by individuals, by families, by nations, by the whole human family. The warning of Pius XII still rings in our ears: *Nothing is lost by peace; everything may be lost by war* (Radio Broadcast, August 24, 1939).

119. We, for Our part, will not cease to pray God to bless these labors so that they may lead to fruitful results.

In the next four paragraphs, the Holy Father returns once again to a favorite concern of his: the obligation of the economically well developed nations to help those that are poor and underdeveloped. This insistence of the Pope should not surprise us for he is "the Holy Father," the father of all men, and most especially the father of the poor and abandoned. So he continues:

121. Because all men are joined together by reason of their common origin, their redemption by Christ, and their supernatural destiny, and are called to form one Christian family, We appealed in the Encyclical *Mater et Magistra* to economically developed nations to come to the aid of those which were in process of development.

We have seen this already but the Pope wants to repeat it over again to remind all men that they are truly brothers under God and because of this that they are "their brothers' keepers." For Christians there is another and greater reason: they are called to help one another because all men have

been loved and saved by Jesus Christ. No matter
who and where they are, Christ loved them and
died for each and every one of them. We imitate
Christ when we love and aid others with all of
our strength and energy.

122. We are greatly consoled to see how widely that
appeal has been favorably received; and We are con-
fident that even more so in the future it will contribute to the end that the poorer countries, in as
short a time as possible, will arrive at that degree of
economic development which will enable every citizen to live in conditions in keeping with his human
dignity.

There can be little doubt that the Pope is refer-
ring to the aid given by the United States since
the end of World War II. In the past few decades
we have given over ninety-eight billion dollars
worth of aid to the countries of the world. We can
well be proud of that for never in history has any
nation given so much in material wealth. The
Pope praises this generosity but he also adds: We
must not stop now for there are too many poor
and starving people in the world today. We must
not discontinue this aid so necessary to the world
today, says the Holy Father. "Foreign aid," as
we call it, must continue to flow. It is a work
both of justice and love. These are brothers we
are helping, not strangers or people who have
nothing to do with us. No true Christian could
oppose foreign aid.

123. But it is never sufficiently repeated that the cooperation, to which reference has been made, should

be effected with the greatest respect for the liberty of the countries being developed, for these must realize that they are primarily responsible, and that they are the principal artisans in the promotion of their own economic development and social progress.

We have already spoken of colonialism, or the control of one country by another. This can be accomplished in many different ways. One country, for example, could march soldiers into another country and conquer it. Another country can control a weaker one by economic means. For instance, when someone wants to borrow some money from me, I can say to him, "Do what I want or you will not receive the money you need." A rich nation can also do the same thing to a poor nation dependent on the rich nation for money and supplies necessary to its own development. The Holy Father warns the developed nations not to do this because, in effect, this is simply another form of colonialism. When a country gives aid, it must do so in a pure way with no strings attached. We must aid our brothers all over the world simply because they are our brothers. This does not mean that our own self-interest should be totally absent; it only means that in our relationship with other nations, self-interest must not be first and foremost. The Holy Father continues along this same line when he says:

124. Our Predecessor Pius XII already proclaimed that *in the field of a new order founded on moral principles, there is no room for violation of freedom, integrity and security of other nations, no matter*

what may be their territorial extension or their capacity for defence. It is inevitable that the powerful States, by reason of their greater potential and their power, should pave the way in the establishment of economic groups comprising not only themselves but also smaller and weaker States as well. It is nevertheless indispensable that in the interests of the common good they, as all others, should respect the rights of those smaller States to political freedom, to economic development and to the adequate protection, in the case of conflicts between nations, of that neutrality which is theirs according to the natural, as well as international, law. In this way, and in this way only, will they be able to obtain a fitting share of the common good, and assure the material and spiritual welfare of their people (Cf. Radio Broadcast, Christmas Eve, 1941).

And the Holy Father goes on to insist once again on the obligation of the richer nations to aid the poorer ones:

125. It is vitally important, therefore, that the wealthier States, in providing varied forms of assistance to the poorer, should respect the moral values and ethnic characteristics peculiar to each, and also that they should avoid any intention of political domination. *If this be done, it will help much toward shaping a community of all nations, wherein each one, aware of its rights and duties, will have regard for the prosperity of all* (John XXIII, *Mater et Magistra*).

In our United States there seems to be a growing opposition to the idea of "foreign aid." It is quite true that our government must see to it that all of this money is spent correctly and that it truly helps the underdeveloped peoples themselves and not just the rich businessmen of various countries; after all, the citizen must work hard for every tax dollar he gives to the government. But there are many people who oppose the whole concept of foreign aid because it costs too much. The argument only demonstrates the selfishness of some Americans—last year Americans made 600 billion dollars in income. Certainly it is selfish to say that we cannot afford foreign aid. Moreover this argument is in direct conflict with what the Holy Father stated in his other encyclical letter, *Mater et Magistra* when he said:

Perhaps the most pressing question of our day concerns the relationship between economically advanced commonwealths and those that are in the process of development. The former enjoy the conveniences of life; the latter experience dire poverty. . . . The nations that enjoy a sufficiency and abundance of everything may not overlook the plight of other nations whose citizens experience such domestic problems that they are . . . not able to enjoy basic human rights. . . . "We all share responsibility for the fact that populations are undernourished. Therefore, it is necessary to arouse a sense of responsibility in individuals and generally with the world's goods" (par. 157-158).

This calls for greater sacrifice and effort on our part. Hence, "It is hoped that in the future, the richer countries will make greater and greater efforts to provide developing countries with aid designated to promote science, technology and economic life" (*ibid.* par. 165).

With this, the Holy Father ends part three.

DISCUSSION QUESTIONS

1. Is there any law governing the relationship between States?
2. Why can't a ruler forget about his conscience when he is in public office?
3. What do we mean when we say that a State has a right to self-development?
4. Is there any such thing as a "master-race"? Explain.
5. What is the evil of propaganda?
6. Why is it so dangerous today to settle differences between States by means of war?
7. What is overpopulation? What are some of the solutions to this problem?
8. Why are there political refugees in our day?
9. What are the reasons for disarmament? What is the danger facing mankind by a buildup of arms?
10. Why should we help underdeveloped countries of the world? Do we have a moral obligation to do so?

PART 4
Relationship
Of Men And Of States
With The World Community

WE NOW COME to what is perhaps the most important part of the Pope's encyclical. In it, the Holy Father says that the time has come to form one world community with an authority that will promote the common good of the whole human race. We have already seen what the common good is; now we must extend it to include all men. Since there is now no authority that can promote the total good of all men, regardless of their native land, the Pope says that the time has come to create and strengthen such an authority.

This should not be something new to us Christians. After all, we are one family already since God created us all with the same nature and the same destiny. We are all brothers before we are Americans or Japanese or Russians. Therefore, an authority having the power to protect men all over the world is not a strange idea to Catholics. We of the Catholic Church are from every country of the world, yet we belong to one Church and to one faith. This does not alter the fact that we are also members of a smaller diocese. The two are parts of one great reality: the Church. So, too, in the political order. That I am an American is fine, but this does not detract from the fact that I also belong to the whole human race.

I belong to both communities and I owe them both my loyalty and my love.

The modern world, moreover, has been brought together and condensed somewhat, by communications, travel, and science. Men are more and more dependent on each other and because of this, some authority should be created to insure that these ever increasing relationships are governed and ruled in justice. Only a world-wide authority with power can do this today.

Since all these things are so, says the Holy Father, it is the moral obligation of all men (especially Catholics) to work for the creation of such a community. If something pertains to the moral law, as we have seen, it is God's will and no Catholic can really be a Catholic unless he attempts to live accordingly. This is what the Pope will discuss in this section of the encyclical.

130. Recent progress of science and technology has profoundly affected human beings and influenced men to work together and live as one family. There has been a great increase in the circulation of goods, of ideas and of persons from one country to another, so that relations have become closer between individuals, families and intermediate associations belonging to different political communities, and between the public authorities of those communities. At the same time the interdependence of national economies has grown deeper, one becoming progressively more closely related to the other, so that they become, as it were, integral parts of the one world economy. Likewise the social progress, order, security and peace of each country are necessarily con-

nected with the social progress, order, security and peace of all other countries.

The Holy Father first gives the reasons why men have become more closely related in this 20th-century world. What are some of these reasons?

The Advances of Science. Distances are relatively smaller today. We can get anywhere in the world in a matter of hours. The astronauts have even circled the earth in eighty minutes. Sickness and disease as well as floods and droughts are being more easily controlled throughout the world. As a matter of fact, the very growth of science itself has become international and many countries contribute to its progress with their mutual endeavors.

Economic Life. Trade today is world wide. The European common market is an example of how men can cooperate in trade agreements. Nations are more and more dependent on other nations for mutual economic prosperity. The price of coffee in Brazil can affect the whole world market and economy. No nation today is economically independent.

Travel and Culture. We can acquire firsthand knowledge about other people and their traditions through wide reading that is so available today as well as through travel. In addition student exchange programs have helped us to understand each other better and to appreciate each other's gifts and values.

Modern War. No nation can live isolated from danger. Since distances are shorter (Intercontinental Ballistic Missiles) and destruction so great (nuclear bombs) we must join forces both in common defense as well as in mutual efforts to promote peace in this world.

Thus, the Holy Father clearly shows how much of a real human family men have become and how much they have come to depend on each other in today's modern world. Thus, the Pope goes on to the next point in his development:

131. At the present day no political community is able to pursue its own interests and develop itself in isolation, because the degree of its prosperity and development is a reflection and a component part of the degree of prosperity and development of all the other political communities.

This conclusion follows from what the Holy Father said above. What authority will regulate relations between individual states if, as we have seen, all nations are equal in dignity? What authority will see to it that every nation, whether it is large or small, will always be assured of justice in its dealings with other nations? At present, there is no authority of a world-wide force and this is the reason why men must join together to establish and then strengthen such a world-wide authority. The Pope gives still another reason for this when he says that:

132. The unity of the human family has always existed, because its members were human beings all

equal by virtue of their natural dignity. Hence there will always exist the objective need to promote, in sufficient measure, the universal common good, that is, the common good of the entire human family.

We have already seen that all men are brothers and that what happens to one (or one nation) is of importance to all of the rest—or at least it should be. Since this is so, men are brothers and must always seek to act together in a spirit of brotherly cooperation.

All these problems are international. That is, they concern many nations all over the world. One nation simply cannot do it alone. This is not because individual nations have bad or evil intentions. On the contrary, most nations have good will. The reason is rather that these problems are too complicated, too big for any one nation to solve by itself. Nations must cooperate to solve these problems under an authority which will have as its principal duty or job, to promote and safeguard the rights, independence and duties of all nations of the human race. As the Pope says:

134. As a result of the far-reaching changes which have taken place in the relations within the human community, the universal common good gives rise to problems that are very grave, complex and extremely urgent, especially as regards security and world peace. On the other hand, the public authorities of the individual nations—being placed as they are on a footing of equality one with the other—no matter how much they multiply their meetings or sharpen their wits in efforts to draw up new juridical instru-

ments, they are no longer capable of facing the task of finding an adequate solution to the problems mentioned above. And this is not due to a lack of good will or of a spirit of enterprise, but because their authority lacks suitable force.

The only conclusion can be the development of a world-wide authority that can do the job. The Holy Father says this in very clear terms when he says:

137. Today the universal common good poses problems of world-wide dimensions, which cannot be adequately tackled or solved except by the efforts of public authorities endowed with a wideness of powers, structure and means of the same proportions: that is, of public authorities which are in a position to operate in an effective manner on a world-wide basis. The moral order itself, therefore, demands that such a form of public authority be established.

The Holy Father is very concise in asking for a moral order that calls for such a community of world-wide authority. It is not simply the wish of the Holy Father; it is the will of God that we all work together for the establishment of such an order.

There are some men who say that we owe our country our first and only loyalty. They say that we owe nothing to other peoples and other nations. Our first and greatest love and loyalty must be to our own country.

There is some truth in what they say. Loyalty to our country and its history is what we call the virtue of patriotism. We are justly proud of our history, of our accomplishments as a nation. Yet, there is a still greater loyalty to our brothers all over the world. We must see to it that they, too, are protected and advanced. However, we can never sacrifice or give up one loyalty for another. The two must be united into a single loyalty to our brothers of the whole human race. We should never think that we have to choose between the two. We must not choose but try to coordinate the two obligations to our country and to all men. The Holy Father urges us to do so because it is the will of God for us.

The Holy Father now goes on to give the basis of this world-wide authority when he says:

139. Like the common good of individual political communities, so too the universal common good cannot be determined except by having regard to the human person. Therefore, the public authority of the world community, too, must have as its fundamental objective the recognition, respect, safeguard ing and promotion of the rights of the human person; this can be done by direct action when required, or by creating on a world scale an environment in which the public authorities of the individual polit- ical communities can more easily carry out their spe- cific functions.

Once again, the Holy Father returns to the rock-bottom foundation for every political so- ciety. What is true for the individual States is just as true for the world-wide authority that the Holy Father has been talking about. The rights and freedoms of the human person are the heart and soul of this authority. Without this, we will only have tyranny on a world-wide basis and that would be very serious. And the Holy Father gives specifics. He goes on to mention what he has in mind for the job. He singles out for praise the *Universal Declaration of Human Rights* when he says:

143. An act of the highest importance performed by the United Nations Organization was the *Universal Declaration of Human Rights,* approved in the General Assembly of December 10, 1948. In the preamble to that Declaration, the recognition of and respect for those rights and respective liberties is proclaimed as an ideal to be pursued by all peoples and all countries.

In it, the nations declare that the State exists for men and not man for the State; man has freedoms and liberties that no one may take from him such as freedom of religion, of the press, of travel, of writing, and reading, etc. It is much like our own Bill of Rights. This is important because at least a beginning has been made in recognizing that these rights belong to all men. Catholics, the Holy Father says, must cooperate in any possible way to help make real this *Universal Declaration of Human Rights.* To do so is a great act of charity and love for our fellow man.

But the Holy Father clearly shows that this world authority is not to destroy individual nations but rather to help them develop harmoniously with each other. In other words the job of the world-wide authority is to protect each individual and each nation in the world through justice, not to take the place of these countries. So the Pope says:

141. The public authority of the world community is not intended to limit the sphere of action of the public authority of the individual political community, much less to take its place. On the contrary, its purpose is to create, on a world basis, an environment in which the public authorities of each political community, its citizens and intermediate associations, can carry out their tasks, fulfill their duties and exercise their rights with greater security.

Thus, this world authority is a protection and a safeguard for all nations and peoples whether they are large or small. The individual nations must take care of their own citizens; this is their domain. But when it comes to the relations between one country and another, then the world authority must regulate things by laws and if necessary, by police force. In this way, wars and conflicts will be avoided and justice will prevail.

But the Pope does not stop there. He does not leave us "up in the air." He does not just repeat generalities without giving us something solid and real. In the tradition of Pope Pius XII, he names the *United Nations* as the beginning of the world authority that he has in mind. This is what the Pope says:

142. As is known, the United Nations Organization (UN) was established on June 26, 1945, and to it there were subsequently added Intergovernmental Agencies with extensive international tasks in the economic, social, cultural, educational and health

fields. The United Nations Organization had as its essential purpose the maintenance and consolidation of peace between peoples, fostering between them friendly relations, based on the principles of equality, mutual respect, and varied forms of cooperation in every sector of human society.

This is important. Some Christians and even some Catholics have not approved of the U.N. Such is not the case with the Holy Father. He sees in it a hope for peace and a means of exercising the world authority of which he has been speaking. It is the best authority man has developed so far and he encourages Catholics not only to join it but to cooperate with it in all of its endeavors to bring about peace in our world. Pope Pius XII said the same thing especially with respect to disarmament. In an earlier document Pope Pius XII says:

The U.N. ought to have the right and power of forestalling all military intervention of one state into another whatever be the pretext under which it is affected and also the right of power of assuming by means of a sufficient police force, the safeguarding of order in the state which is threatened. . . . We desire to see the authority of the U.N. strengthened, especially for effecting general disarmament . . . under the strict obligation of international law. Only the U.N. at present is in a position to exact such observance (*The Pope Speaks*, 3, 331-338).

Let us simply say that support of the U.N. and its objectives is a very serious matter for all Catholics. We *must* cooperate with it in every way we can do so. Cardinal Montini (now Pope Paul

VI) said the same thing: "How many Catholics continue to shut themselves within the narrow confines of . . . nationalism incompatible with courageous effort to start a world community *demanded* by recent Popes." For Catholics, the words could not be clearer.

The Holy Father recognizes that the U.N. is not perfect. This is very true. But if it is not perfect that is no reason why we should deny it our support. On the contrary, this is all the more reason why Catholics should attempt to improve it. That is why the Pope says:

144. Some objections and reservations were raised regarding certain points in the Declaration. There is no doubt, however, that the document represents an important step on the path toward the juridical-political organization of the world community. For in it, in most solemn form, the dignity of a person is acknowledged to all human beings; and as a consequence there is proclaimed, as a fundamental right, the right of free movement in the search for truth and in the attainment of moral good and of justice, and also the right to a dignified life, while other rights connected with those mentioned are likewise proclaimed.

But notice the following paragraph. He does not condemn the U.N. because it is imperfect; instead he utters a virtual prayer that it will become all the more perfect. There can be no doubt that he is appealing to Catholics above all to try to make it all the more perfect when he says:

145. It is Our earnest wish that the United Nations Organization—in its structure and in its means—may

become ever more equal to the magnitude and nobility of its tasks. May the day soon come when every human being will find therein an effective safeguard for the rights which derive directly from his dignity as a person, and which are therefore universal, inviolate and inalienable rights. This is all the more to be hoped for since all human beings, as they take an ever more active part in the public life of their own political communities, are showing an increasing interest in the affairs of all peoples, and are becoming more consciously aware that they are living members of a universal family of mankind.

With this great prayer and desire, the Holy Father ends this section of his encyclical.

DISCUSSION QUESTIONS

1. What are the reasons for men becoming more dependent on each other?
2. Can individual States solve all the problems of the modern world? Why not?
3. Will the world authority of which the Pope speaks take over all the governments of the world?
4. What is the task of this world authority and what is its solid foundation?
5. What act does the Holy Father single out for great praise?
6. What does the Holy Father think of the U.N.?
7. Should Catholics try to get out of the U.N.?

PART 5
Pastoral
Exhortations

BEFORE FINISHING his message to "all men of good will," the Holy Father makes some suggestions especially for Catholics. He instructs them about how they are to work together with "all men of good will" to better the society in which they live. When you stop to think of it, to work together with someone on a common job is one of the best ways to promote friendship. Pope John wants all Catholics to develop a deep friendship with these men. We must always remember that there are many men of good will, who are pleasing to God and doing His will, even though they do not belong to our Catholic faith. The important thing is that good things get done in society and it makes little difference who does that good. Catholics have not always been co-operative in this way in the past, but these are different times with both Pope John XXIII and Pope Paul VI revolutionizing the Church from top to bottom. There is a lot of important work to be done and we must not pay attention to *who* does it; the important thing is that good is being done.

But who is going to have this job of making the teachings of Christ and of the Church known to the modern world? It can only be the Catholic layman because he alone comes into real contact with the modern world. This is what has been called the *lay apostolate* that the Popes have been talking about for the last twenty-five years. It is around this idea that the Holy Father is going to speak in this section of his letter.

146. Once again We deem it opportune to remind Our children of their duty to take an active part in public life, and to contribute toward the attainment of the common good of the entire human family as well as to that of their own political community. Men should endeavor, therefore, in the light of the faith and with the strength of love, to ensure that the various institutions — whether economic, social, cultural or political in purpose — will be such as not to create obstacles, but rather to facilitate the task of improving themselves both in the natural order as well as in the supernatural.

Here the Pope reminds Catholics that they have a duty to take an active part in accomplishing the things he has been talking about. For the Catholic layman, it is part of his real religious duty. We must not restrict our religious duties to Church and the saying of the rosary; these are important but equally important and a direct part of the Christian life is to take part in public life. One cannot be a good Catholic by going to Mass on Sunday and conducting one's business or profession as if Christ did not exist. This is scandalous and against God's will. We must bring Christ's ideas into our places of work as well. It is only the layman who can do this. As the Pope says:

147. Nevertheless, in order to imbue civilization with sound principles and enliven it with the spirit of the gospel, it is not enough to be illumined with the gift of faith and enkindled with the desire of forwarding a good cause. For this end it is necessary to take an active part in the various organizations and influence them from within.

Thus, the Holy Father directly appeals to laymen to enter the fields that he discussed earlier in his letter. One must have faith as a guide, so that we know what Christ wants of us. But this is not sufficient; we must enter into society, into business, professions, industry, science, education etc. to "transform" them, to fill them with the very ideals of Christ. Would it not be terrible to say that Christ does not care about these things? Since it was Christ who created them all, it would be actually sinful to say that Christ was unconcerned. "All was made by Him and for Him" says St. Paul (Col. 1:16). Since everything belongs to Christ, we have a definite obligation to see to it that everything in this world is directed to Him. But how is this to be done? The Pope gives the answer in the next paragraph when he says:

148. But since our present age is one of outstanding scientific and technical progress and excellence, one will not be able to enter these organizations and work effectively from within unless he is scientifically competent, technically capable and skilled in the practice of his own profession.

* * * * *

150 For this end it is certainly necessary that human

beings carry on their own temporal activities in accordance with the laws governing them and following the methods corresponding to their nature. But at the same time it is also necessary that they should carry on those activities as acts within the moral order: therefore, as the exercise or vindication of a right, as the fulfillment of a duty or the performance of a service, as a positive answer to the providential design of God directed to our salvation. In other words, it is necessary that human beings, in the intimacy of their own consciences, should so live and act in their temporal lives as to create a synthesis between scientific, technical and professional elements on the one hand, and spiritual values on the other.

Once again, the concept of Pope John XXIII is awesome. As we have said, everything belongs to Christ because He created it. But He wants man to cooperate with Him in redeeming all that He has created. In the beginning, says the Bible, God created heaven and earth. God then placed man upon this earth to develop it *as God's representative*. Man has been given a task or commission by God to develop what God gave him in creation. Therefore, the work of man here on earth (no matter what it is) is a cooperation by man with God. Science, industry, education are all tasks given to man by God. The lawmaker who makes just laws is doing God's work; the person who builds bridges and homes, etc., is doing God's work; the astronomer and the physicist are doing God's work. We can begin to see what we meant when we said that science, industry, etc. cannot contradict our Christian faith. On the contrary, as the Pope points out, since God has created both the world of nature and the world of faith, no contradiction between the two is possible.

But this is the difficulty: science, industry, etc. are all good because God created them and has given them to man to develop. Yet, they can be used both for good and for evil. Nuclear energy, for example, can be used for great good as a new source of energy; but it can also be used to wipe man off the face of the earth. The Holy Father says that this can be remedied by one single solution and to achieve it we need the light of faith and of God's moral truths to guide us toward a just use of this world's goods. All created things were created for man's good and God's greater glory, but they can be used well only when man follows God's will. For this we need the light of faith and the moral principles which the Holy Father has outlined both in this encyclical letter as well as in the former one that he wrote before this one, *Mater et Magistra*. Therefore, it is very important to know what the Church teaches on all of these subjects and we can only obtain that information by studying the social teachings of the Church. As the Pope says:

149. We desire to call attention to the fact that scientific competence, technical capacity and professional experience, although necessary, are not of themselves sufficient to elevate the relationships of society to an order that is genuinely human: that is, to an order whose foundation is truth, whose measure and objective is justice; whose driving force is love, and whose method of attainment is freedom.

This has not always been the case, not even in Catholic circles. Many Catholics did not recognize the unity between their faith and their work in the world. And because they did not realize how to obtain this unity, many thought that religion was for old women and children — not for men with a thinking head on their shoulders. How wrong these Christians and Catholics were is proven by the fact that the Holy Father, time and time again, shows that both man's faith and his work in the world are united in the one act of faith. Everything must be seen as God sees it. That is why the Holy Father says:

152. It is beyond question that in the creation of those institutions many contributed and continue to contribute who were believed to be and who consider themselves Christians; and without doubt, in part at least, they were and are. How does one explain this? It is Our opinion that the explanation is to be found in an inconsistency in their minds between religious belief and their action in the temporal sphere. It is necessary, therefore, that their interior unity be re-established, and that in their temporal activity faith should be present as a beacon to give light, and charity as a force to give life.

The next paragraph shows us how important the Holy Father considers this social teaching of the Catholic Church. It should be taught to children even during the early days of grammar school. This is why he says:

153. It is Our opinion, too, that the above-mentioned inconsistency between the religious faith, in

those who believe, and their activities in the temporal sphere, results—in great part if not entirely—from the lack of a solid Christian education. Indeed, it happens in many quarters and too often that there is no proportion between scientific training and religious instruction: the former continues and is extended until it reaches higher degrees, while the latter remains at elementary level. It is indispensable, therefore, that in the training of youth, education should be complete and without interruption: namely, that in the minds of the young, religious values should be cultivated and the moral conscience refined, in a manner to keep pace with the continuous and ever more abundant assimilation of scientific and technical knowledge. And it is indispensable too that they be instructed regarding the proper way to carry out their actual tasks.

The Holy Father then tells us that we must never be satisfied with the work we have accomplished. There are so many injustices in our world that even if we worked day and night to overcome them, there would still remain a very great deal to be done. As long as there is one person hungry in this world, as long as one person suffers injustice in any way, we can never rest peacefully. That is, at least, the way Christ would look at it and that is the way the Holy Father wants us to look at the situation in our world:

156. In fact, all human beings ought rather to reckon that what has been accomplished is but little in comparison with what remains to be done: because organs of production, trade unions, associations, professional organizations, insurance systems, legal systems, political regimes, institutions for cultural,

health, recreational or athletic purposes—these must all be adjusted to the era of the atom and of the conquest of space, an era which the human family has already entered, wherein it has commenced its new advance toward limitless horizons.

Now the Holy Father goes on to describe the principles that Catholics can follow in cooperation with other men of good will. He says:

157. The doctrinal principles outlined in this document derive from or are suggested by requirements inherent in human nature itself, and are, for the most part, dictates of the natural law. They provide Catholics, therefore, with a vast field in which they can meet and come to an understanding both with Christians separated from this Apostolic See, and also with human beings who are not enlightened by faith in Jesus Christ, but who are endowed with the light of reason and with a natural and operative honesty. *On such occasions, those who profess Catholicism must take special care to be consistent and not compromise in matters wherein the integrity of religion or morals would suffer harm. Likewise, in their conduct they should weigh the opinions of others with fitting courtesy and not measure everything in the light of their own interests. They should be prepared to join sincerely in doing whatever is naturally good or conducive to good* (John XXIII, *Mater Et Magistra*).

It is possible because all men—Catholics and non-Catholics — possess the same human nature created by God. Each man has the gift of a mind (or reason) and a free will. With these he can reason; he can find out what God wants him to do. We have stated before that all of nature is

like a book in which we can read the will of God.
This is true and we can read God's will because
we all have a reason or mind. Therefore, for the
social good of society and of other men, we
should cooperate in what we call the natural
good. What is this? It means that in such things
as just laws, civil rights, anti-discrimination, foreign aid, the U.N., etc., we can work together with
all men of good will because they, too, by their
reason, can see that these things are good, pleasing to God and need to be done.

It is evident that all of this and even more is
possible between Catholic and Protestant as well
as Orthodox. Even more than other men of good
will, Protestants are closer to us for the simple
reason that they love and believe in Jesus Christ.
They share Christ's divine life with us and therefore we should miss no opportunity to cooperate
and work together with them in all of the problems that the Pope has mentioned throughout
this encyclical letter. As a matter of fact, this
kind of action will help bring about the complete
unity of all Christians for which we pray so often.

The Holy Father now makes a careful distinction when he says:

158. Moreover, one must never confuse error and
the person who errs, not even when there is question
of error or inadequate knowledge of truth in the
moral or religious field. The person who errs is always and above all a human being, and he retains
in every case his dignity as a human person; and he
must be always regarded and treated in accordance

with that lofty dignity. Besides, in every human being, there is a need that is congenial to his nature and never becomes extinguished, compelling him to break through the web of error and open his mind to the knowledge of truth. And God will never fail to act on his interior being, with the result that a person, who at a given moment of his life lacked the clarity of faith or even adheres to erroneous doctrines, can at a future date learn and believe the truth. Meetings and agreements in the various sectors of daily life, between believers and those who do not believe or believe insufficiently because they adhere to error, can be occasions for discovering truth and paying homage to it.

It is so easy to confuse the person who errs and the error itself. We must always hate and detest all error no matter where we find it. But we must be very, very careful. Under no circumstance can we hate the person who commits an error. We are never permitted to hate the Communist or the Russian or the criminal. This is very easy to do and many do it today. As Catholics and as Christians we must love all men and respect them. To do injustice to them (even though we know they would do the same to us if they could) makes us no better than any one of them. We would be overcome by the evil that we ourselves want to overcome. It is only in loving and in serving other men to prove that love that we can overcome our enemies. And our intention should be to overcome them not in the sense of destroying them but in the sense of converting them. When you kill someone, the only thing you have proven is that you have greater force. When you convert someone, you prove the power of love and truth over hate and mistrust. This must be our constant endeavor.

We should even admit that some of our enemies' statements are true. Karl Marx, one of the original Communists, erred often; but he was right at least in that he recognized the injustices to the working man and he spoke out against them. That is a lot more than many Christians of that era did. It is an old adage that if you want to learn the truth about yourself, go speak to your enemies. So too with our enemies. We should examine very carefully what they say to see whether there might not be some truth in their statements. The Holy Father says the same thing when he says:

159. It must be borne in mind, furthermore, that neither can false philosophical teachings regarding the nature, origin and destiny of the universe and of man, be identified with historical movements that have economic, social, cultural or political ends, not even when these movements have originated from those teachings and have drawn and still draw inspiration therefrom. For these teachings, once they are drawn up and defined, remain always the same, while the movements, working on historical situations in constant evolution, cannot but be influenced by these latter and cannot avoid, therefore, being subject to changes, even of a profound nature. Besides, who can deny that those movements, in so far as they conform to the dictates of right reason and are interpreters of the lawful aspirations of the human person, contain elements that are positive and deserving of approval?

But we must not be discouraged if things move slowly. This is the way with all change in human affairs—it moves at a slow pace. We must have patience. Yet we must be careful for going slowly must not be used as an excuse to do nothing. Many people, for instance, who say that we must go slowly with a solution to the Negro problem, use this "going slow" as an excuse to do nothing. This is not what the Holy Father means. Thus the Pope says:

162. It must be borne in mind that to proceed gradually is the law of life in all its expressions; therefore in human institutions, too, it is not possible to renovate for the better except by working from within them, gradually. Pius XII proclaimed: *Salvation and justice are not to be found in revolution, but in evolution through concord. Violence has always achieved only destruction, not construction; the kindling of passions, not their pacification; the accumulation of hate and ruin, not the reconciliation of the contending parties. And it has reduced men and parties to the difficult task of rebuilding, after sad experience, on the ruins of discord* (Cf. Allocution on Pentecost, June 13, 1943).

In other words, even if we have to go slowly, we must move, we must do something. The only thing that comes with time alone is old age. As the Holy Father says, we must practice Christian charity in facts and deeds to help our fellow man, not with just a lot of cheap words.

The Holy Father is just a little bit discouraged in this next paragraph. It is a complaint, in a sense, that there are not more who prove their love by trying to bring about what he has been discussing throughout his letter. The reason is simple: if you go out and try to do what the Holy Father wants, you are going to have to suffer for it and there are not many people who want to suffer for Christ. Thus the Pope says:

164. Admittedly, those who are endeavoring to restore the relations of social life according to the criteria mentioned above, are not many; to them We express Our paternal appreciation, and We earnestly invite them to persevere in their work with ever greater zeal. And We are comforted by the hope that their number will increase, especially among Christian believers. For it is an imperative of duty; it is a requirement of love. Every believer in this world of ours must be a spark of light, a center of love, a vivifying leaven amidst his fellow men: and he will be this all the more perfectly the more closely he lives in communion with God in the intimacy of his own soul.

Thus, the Holy Father says, peace is above all the relationship of man with God. It is inside each man who lives, as the Pope says:

165. In fact, there can be no peace between men unless there is peace within each one of them; unless, that is, each one builds up within himself the order wished by God. Hence St. Augustine asks: *Does your soul desire to overcome your lower inclinations? Let it be subject to Him who is on high and it will conquer the lower self: there will be peace in you; true, secure and well-ordered peace. In what does that order consist? God commands the soul; the soul commands the body; and there is nothing more orderly than this.*

Each man and woman must first endeavor to reform his or her own life before he can begin to reform the lives of others in society. There can be no peace in the world unless there is first peace in men's souls for that is where the true trouble lies. Man's greed, impurity, and hate of his fellow man come from his soul and then are imparted to the society in which he lives. Therefore, a man must be first converted within his own soul for only then will he see that God's ways are the ways of understanding, love, and justice.

But man alone cannot do this. He must have help from on high so that the grace of the Holy Spirit can come into the souls of men converting them from their blindness and hatred to His love. Only the grace of God can make men clearly see that they are brothers under God and that they must work together for each other. Only the grace of God can break down the barriers that have separated men and nations for so long. Only the Prince of Peace, Christ, can accomplish these and it is for this that we must continuously pray with all of our hearts and souls. The Holy Father concludes his encyclical with the following beautiful words:

169. For this reason, during these sacred days Our supplication is raised with greater fervor toward Him who by His painful Passion and death overcame sin—the root of discord and the source of sorrows and inequalities—and by His Blood reconciled mankind to the Eternal Father; *For He Himself is our peace, He it is that has made both one . . . And*

*coming He announced the good tidings of peace to
you who were afar off, and of peace to those who
were near* (Eph. 2, 14-17).

171. This is the peace which We implore of Him
with the ardent yearning of Our prayer. May He
banish from the hearts of men whatever might en-
danger peace, may He transform them into witnesses
of truth, justice and brotherly love. May He enlighten the rulers of peoples so that in addition to
their solicitude for the proper welfare of their citizens, they may guarantee and defend the great gift
of peace. Finally, may Christ enkindle the wills of
all, so that they may overcome the barriers that divide, cherish the bonds of mutual charity, understand others, and pardon those who have done them
wrong. By virtue of His action, may all peoples of
the earth become as brothers, and may the most
longed-for peace blossom forth and reign always between them.

DISCUSSION QUESTIONS

1. What does Christ expect of the Catholic
   layman?
2. Does man's work in the world mean anything for Christ?
3. Why must the Catholic take part in public
   life?
4. Should we cooperate with non-Catholics in
   doing good? Why?
5. Why, in the past, have Christians separated
   their religious belief from their temporal
   work in the world?
6. What do we mean when we say that everything belongs to Christ?

7. What is the great danger of modern science separated from faith and Christ?
8. Should we ever be self-satisfied with ourselves? Why not?
9. What distinction should we make between error and the person who errs?
10. What is peace? How will it come about according to the Holy Father?